RV Camping

RV Living for Beginners

book.

By reading this document, the reader agrees that under no
circumstances is the author responsible for any losses, direct
or indirect, which are incurred as a result of the use of
information contained within this document, including, but
not limited to, — errors, omissions, or inaccuracies.

Learn <u>All</u> The Top Secrets To Camping In The Great Outdoors And Make Your First Adventure A <u>Complete</u> Success

I have something very **exciting** to share with you!

<u>**IMAGINE**</u> your first RV camping adventure being an outright victory! This <u>FREE</u> bonus book reveals hidden secrets about creating lasting memories and enjoying lots of fun activities <u>**without**</u> killing your wallet!

Click on the link below **now** to discover that secret for yourself which has been **proven** effective for helping folks gather so many camping pics and getting all their friends jealous! Get it now **because** you deserve to get away from technology and go explore nature!

http://bit.ly/SecretsToCamping

Table of Contents

Preface

"Making a big life change is pretty scary. But, know what's even scarier? Regret."[1]

Several years ago, I remember going through some articles on the Internet and reading about a couple living in an RV so that they could pay off their debts and live a simple life. I remember thinking to myself, "That seems like a cool idea, but I would never be able to live in an RV."

Those were my exact thoughts. I would not be able to leave the comfort of our home, security, a consistent income and Wi-Fi of course. Furthermore, what terrified me was that it might be considered as "less" and that people might judge me for an RV lifestyle.

But fate had chosen otherwise, and I ended up meeting a girl in college who would later turn out to be my wife who would challenge me to dream big and to not worry about what the world thought of me. A couple of years after our marriage and living comfortably in our home in Texas, we reached the crossroads of life where we had a decision to make. It was a decision between living in the comfort of our home and neighborhood like everyone else or to hit the open roads and the wilderness in an RV. We decided a life full of adventure and memories over comfort, and it's made all the difference in

---

[1] https://quotefancy.com/quote/943227/Zig-Ziglar-Making-a-big-life-change-is-pretty-scary-But-know-what-s-even-scarier-Regret

1

the world.

It's not been a fairytale exactly, and we wish we could tell you that there were times when we were scared and doubted our decision and were unsure about the situations we were in. We don't have anything against the house as both my wife and I grew up in cozy homes. After college, all our friends were settling down. But there was nothing inside of us that wanted us to get anywhere near the concept of settling down. We wanted to explore the world. We wanted to climb mountains, bathe in rivers and run like wild animals in the forest.

So there we were, hopping across states in America and we have done a few over 30 states by now. The experience has been beautiful, and there is no other luxury in the world that we would trade it for in this life or another. We've had a roller coaster journey, both metaphorically and literally ever since we set off on this life full of adventure and we would urge you to take it too. Man has been living comfortably in the confined space of his house for ages, and we ended up questioning ourselves if we should follow the same conventions that have been set by our ancestors? Do we need the same routine every day for the rest of our lives or do we get up every morning and live a day which would be completely different than the day we lived yesterday?

Living in an RV is what has taught us about living in the true sense of the word. Out there on the road, the structures of the concrete world begin to collapse. You get camouflaged by nature, and the concepts of race and color vanish. Nature draws you in and gently lets you out. You begin to realize that borders only exist on paper. For once, you learn how to embrace happiness in life without knowing what lies ahead.

And you realize that conventions are for a human-made society. Life is ours in the open as the creator intended it to be.

Part I: Let's Begin

"Here I am, on the road again, here I am, up on the stage

Here I go, playin' star again, there I go, turn the page."[2]

Chapter One: What is it Like to RV Full Time?

Full Time RVing Defined

RV living or living out of a Recreational Vehicle is life designed for those of us who do not want to limit our lifestyle within the carpet space of 4 walls. We've been seeing a life being lived by our parents and others around us, which has a set of rules, a set routine and is basically repeating the same day over and over again every day. It is a safe life and has kept us comfortable for a long time but how long is the question. Living should be about going through new experiences every day, and that is exactly what we will try to achieve through this book.

2

https://en.wikipedia.org/wiki/Turn_the_Page_(Bob_Seger_song)

The decision to leave your comfortable house that is located at a clock's distance from the supermarket, a school, and a hospital isn't an easy one. Moreover, moving away from people you have known for years is even more difficult. If you are thinking about living a full-time RV life, it will help to first be honest with yourself about your motives or intentions to take this step and then plan the transition accordingly.

Most importantly, you should know why you want to leave the conventional way of life and move into an RV. There are several reasons why people feel overwhelmed by a routine life and want something different than the conventional life, which challenges their existence, but before doing so, you should be able to justify this and verbalize it to your own conscience and immediate family about your decision to choose this lifestyle.

If you are a businessman who travels regularly and stays in

random hotels away from family, or if you primarily have a digital job that does not demand a fixed traditional workplace, or if you are just trying to save money by living a simple life with necessities fulfilled, or if you are just an adventure seeker who wants to take the detour from the highway of a regular life; all that factored in with your current employment/living/emotional situation should help you decide what you are hoping to get as returns from this lifestyle, before taking the leap of faith into becoming a full-time RVer.

Considering by now you have decided to move into living a full-time RV life, let's have an honest list down of the upsides and downsides to being a full-time RVer.

Let's start by talking about the positives of an RV life.

You realize that you can live in a small space. For those of you who have a relatively small RV unit and are concerned about how much can be fit inside it, you will find out that there is still a lot of space in there and that you require less space than you had initially thought you might need. Even after you pack up the essentials and place them all in there, you'll be surprised to see that you will still have some extra room.

Given the limited amount of space you have, the chances of you accumulating possessions that you do not really need tend to become low, saving you money and time and eventually reducing the stress of them being damaged or stolen.

Next, for times you are at an RV park and have your full hookups, you realize that it is not that different from living in an actual concrete house. You have constant electricity, constant supply of water and you don't even have to worry about dumping your sewer waste since you are connected to everything. RV parks are also very close to nature as there's a lot of green around and a lot of fresh air to breathe in which you wouldn't typically find around an apartment in a city. It gives you the sense of a State Park or a Campground instead of just a parking lot with chaos all around.

Life also becomes more about living offline than on the Internet. You are out on open roads and in open parks resulting in more socializing. You find yourself asking for directions, and at other times you are the one giving them. You will find yourself looking up for RV meetups and making friends more than ever before. Connections will be quick, but deeper than the ones you had in the life you had in your fixed apartment. You will feel a sense of community stronger than that you felt in the neighborhood you used to live in. RVers will come and go as they have their life to get on with too, but you will find yourself being in touch; always. In the words of the rock band Metallica, "So close, no matter how far. Couldn't be much more from the heart."

The Pros and Cons of Being a Full-Timer

And of course, living in an RV is not a fairytale and is therefore accompanied by its own set of cons. We'd not like to call them cons but additional responsibilities for living a healthy RV life.

The primary advice we would have for you for an RV life is to keep a check on weather and be ready for all kinds of weather since you are literally going to be a part of the entire world and what nature has in store for you. So you need to be on your feet and need to plan your next move in accordance to the weather.

Pest control is next up in line. You and your RV will be exposed to all kinds of environments, which will extend free invitations to different kinds of pests. The base of innate pest control is removing the root cause that is usually a food source. This would include tasks like sweeping the crumbs immediately after a meal, ensuring that the dishes are done regularly, keeping the garbage covered and controlling it from piling up by taking it out regularly. In addition to this, you need to control the vulnerable points outside your RV, which are prone to intrusions from pests. This can be done using simple techniques such as deploying sticky traps at all of the entry points outside and under your RV.

Electromagnetic fields are going to be your next concern. It does not seem like a problem in your day-to-day life but can be harmful in the long run. RVs are a box of metal in the end and can serve as amplifiers to electromagnetic fields. Our advice, in this case, would be to use all electronic devices that operate on EMFs viz. Use your cellphone, Bluetooth, Wi-Fi as sparingly as possible while you are inside your RV. Studies published in Environmental Research journals claimed that the use of cell phone or Bluetooth devices inside a vehicle amplified the radiation by more than 350%. It is also advisable to keep all electronic devices unplugged while not in use, as this will keep the radiation risks low and also cut down the chances of an unwanted fire.

We have comfortably neglected dust in fixed apartments, let alone in an RV. It is scary to see that we conveniently neglect the health hazards caused by dust to human life. But we would like to tell you that dust contains a lot of microbes with chemical contaminants, fungi and all kinds of bacteria, which are more than enough to damage the human body's reproductive organs in the long run. Therefore, dust control becomes an integral part of your daily routine while living full time in an RV. Regular dusting using a microfiber cloth, avoiding wearing shoes inside the RV, vacuuming the RV regularly and using a good RV air intake filter are some of the small things you can do to ensure a dust-free RV life.

Life on the go also means having a lot of backup power that mainly will come from batteries. It is a noted behavior that a person will have his batteries scattered around all other items. Leaving batteries unattended may seem like a small thing but may lead to hazardous events such as a fire. The simplest thing to do is to have an inexpensive battery organizer to store these batteries.

Since you are in the open, you cannot neglect the possibilities of thefts or break-ins. You will not be in a typical neighborhood that is under CCTV surveillance or a phone call away from calling the cops. Therefore, it becomes important that the physical security of your RV is in place to prevent instances of thefts or break-ins. Parking the RV in well-lit areas, and having a deadbolt to lock your doors are a few precautionary measures you can take towards security. Since you are living in a small closed environment, you have to think about the gases that will be produced in that little eco-system on account of your life there. Hydrogen Sulphide and Carbon Monoxide are the two gases that will be common in an RV lifestyle.

When organic matter breaks down, it leads to the production of the Hydrogen Sulphide gas which gives off a pungent odor like that of rotten eggs. Continuous exposure can result in unconsciousness and can eventually be fatal as well. Since this is a sewage gas, you need to ensure that you have your sewage vents in place and do invest in a good sewage vent cap at all times and replace it at regular intervals.

Partial or incomplete combustion of hydrocarbons leads to the formation of Carbon Monoxide. Combustion appliances should not be a part of tiny spaces, but you cannot avoid them while living the RV camping life. Ensure that your RV has a detector installed to detect these harmful gases. Also, these detectors will only detect when the levels of these gases reach a hazardous stage. Therefore, always, trust your nose too and take appropriate measures when you smell something unusual.

Living In a House On Wheels Compared to Living In a Sticks and Bricks House

The biggest difference is that you have control over your view as you have a mobile home. You are not limited to having the same view every day. You also get to choose your climate. You could experience winters when you'd normally be having summers or vice-versa. You could not have this if you were living in a typical apartment unless you kept relocating.

Other small things need your attention too at least in the initial days before you get used to your RV completely. Given that you are living in a house on wheels, it will not be as stable as your concrete apartment and will shake around when there's any movement. So if you are sharing the space with one or more people, you will need to be conscious and alert about how your movement may affect the other person's activities. Let's say that you have another person, maybe your wife or a partner who is doing any activity with a sharp object like a pair of scissors, you need to be careful about your movements such that they do not result into them hurting themselves. If your RV is equipped with a washer and dryer that could also lead to the RV shaking a lot, and therefore, you need to keep such situations in mind.

Your RV will not have a disposal system, and you have to be careful about the garbage. You don't want any of your garbage going down to the grey tank as that can lead to health hazards.

Most affordable RVs do not come with a dishwasher. So, it's a good idea to use minimal utensils for your meals and consider hand washing the dishes and utensils to avoid any food clogging up in your grey tank.

RV space is very limited as compared to a full-fledged apartment. So, you will have to compromise on privacy when you have guests around. You have to be prepared to share your space with people who will be visiting you and if and when you decide to have kids as well.

Wi-Fi is mediocre in almost all RV parks, as you will have several other RVers sharing the network. Having an unlimited data plan with a wireless provider like AT&T would be a better alternative than using the publicly available Internet which will turn out to be disappointing 99 percent of times. But there is a silver lining to not having Internet easily available at your fingers. You will start getting out more often to appreciate nature and will find alternative and enjoyable activities which will eventually lead to you living a more wholesome life.

The weather will play an important role in making you realize the difference between your apartment and living inside an RV. For example, in the event of a hailstorm, you will not be able to hear each other while living inside an RV and may have to shout on top of your voices to communicate at the time.

Something that you don't have to think about when you are living in an apartment and has been mentioned in the pros and cons earlier is the sewer. When you are living in an RV, you are always thinking about the sewer. It's probably one of the least fun aspects of full-time RVing, but you have to deal with the grey and black tanks.

Another important difference is the mortgage and rent. When you have an apartment, and you sign a lease, your mortgage payment or rent payment is going to be the same throughout your lifetime; however, when you have an RV, you get to have control over that. It is very flexible depending upon the RV Park you're living in and the services that you are opting in for.

Since you are in a mobile home, there's a lot of traveling happening in your life. You get to see more of the world, explore new regions and mingle with various cultures. You get to taste local cuisine too for a minimal cost if you have social skills to mingle with the local people; however, all this is accompanied by a bucket of daily tasks. You need to have daily checks on tires, the gray and black tanks, other common moving parts of the RV and working on new places to stay and the list goes on. Also meeting all the wonderful people every time you are at a new location and then having to leave them can become difficult. Attachments are hard to break, but you will have to get comfortable with this cycle of life once you become a full-time RVer.

Self-Assessment: Is RVing Life The Right Life For You?

1. Are you attached to your family? This includes people whom you've known your entire life up until today like your parents, siblings, etc.

2. Are you a person who is accepting of changes in life?

3. Are you comfortable living in a parking lot or a stranger's backyard?

4. Are you comfortable with rationing something that you've taken for granted all your life such as water?

5. Are you comfortable making friends with strangers?

6. Are you a decent handyman with knowledge of changing a tire, drilling and installing appliances? If not, are you patient to look it up on sources like Google and Youtube?

7. Are you a cook decent enough to survive long periods on the road depending upon your cooking?

8. Are you comfortable with having a rotating friend base?

9. Does being offline and away from the Internet make you uncomfortable?

10. Are you a person who has to have a bath daily?

Let's do a bit of math and calculate your scores.

Give yourself 5 points for every "yes" on questions 1 to 8 and 1 point for a "no."

Give yourself 5 points for every "no" on questions 9 and 10 and 1 point for a "yes."

If you have someone who you're taking along on this journey, how about you ask him or her to take the test and compare scores with them?

36 to 50 points = Congrats! You are a Full-timer: Get that yellow pages out and start looking for an RV dealer right now!

25 to 35 points = well you're halfway there Part-timer: You might want to give it a try. Take some long trips with your desired company and see what's in store for you.

15 to 24 points = Weekend traveler: Let's get you started by having a few weekend trips until you eventually grow into becoming a full-timer?

10 to 14 points = Homely neighborhood person: Well don't bum yourself out just yet. If everyone would be on the road, what would we do with the traffic situation? Local exploring can be fun too eh?

Chapter Two: Preparing Yourself For The Road Ahead

Are You Financially Prepared?

Needless to say, finance is going to be a very important aspect when you have decided to venture into full-time RVing. RVs can cost between $10,000 and $300,000 depending on the style and features. A moderately appointed camper trailer pulled behind a truck might cost $200,000, while a fifth-wheel may be $40,000. Most motorhome prices usually start around $100,000. We will discuss this in detail in the next section where we will talk about how buying an RV the right way can save thousands of dollars.

If you already have savings, well and good and you can kick start your full-time RV life but if you do not have a decent amount of savings and still aspire to be a full-time RVer, given the expenses, consider having an on-the-go job to take care of the necessary expenses while living the RV life. The following expenses go hand in hand with a full-time RV life, which you need to cross check with your available funds or check if you need to work on the go to fulfill them.

- RV Payment: If you have taken a loan to purchase the RV itself.

- Campground Rent: Campgrounds have flexible rents depending upon the location and services.

- Gas: Huge and variable aspect of RV travel.

- Insurance (Health and Vehicle): Something that cannot be discarded.

- Utilities: Depending on your cooking and the temperature outside, propane is something that you need to look at filling up every month.

- Food/Groceries: Rationing the regular needs of food and groceries.

- Repairs/Maintenance: Includes costs of repairs and maintenance of the RV at regular intervals

- Fun: You will end up spending more than budgeted on some days having fun at expensive restaurants or pubs.

- Miscellaneous Expenses: Unaccounted emergencies.

Your Home and Belongings

If you already own a house that has been paid for in full already, you can think of renting it out, as it will serve as a fixed source of income. This will also keep you secure in case if you ever plan to return from full-time RV living. You will also need to consider the fact that if you rent your home out, you will need to keep a family member or employ someone to look over the maintenance bit of your property. Whatever it is, you cannot leave your home vacant.

If you have a house that is still undergoing mortgage payments, you may want to think about selling it and re-financing it into buying yourself an RV. If you do not have existing savings in your bank account to fund this dream of RV living, it would only make sense to sell everything you own to create a small RV cave comfortable enough to set off. Also with respect to your belongings, you will have to make a choice and take only the essentials with you, which will be bound of by the space restrictions of your new RV life.

When to Start Your Adventure

Is there a right time to start a full-time RV life?

Let's be honest. Being a nomad in today's world is not considered "normal." Also, it took a considerable amount of effort and sweat to reach where you are in life today and to have established yourself. Therefore, to leave all that and start a new life altogether would mean that you start from scratch and will need another iteration of effort and hard work to fulfill the same.

A life that will constantly be keeping you on the go is not necessarily an easy one, but it would be worth it, and you will be content with it. One step a day and you will eventually become an expert at planning it out for your entire life. These tips and tricks would help you transition from a life fixed to an apartment to life on the open road.

Set a Departure Date

Before jumping into the pool of details for your switch, it is very important to set a departure date. It may sound unnecessary, because how can a person say when he will be ready for the RV life?

You don't know. But without a deadline, there would not be any urgency in your head, and this could mean that you will end up procrastinating for the remainder of your life about being on the road. A date makes the planning a serious deal and more real, and certainly more urgent. The date is, therefore, a good motivator to transform your dream into a reality for living that full-time RV life.

The amount of time you will need depends on the kind of life you are living right now. How much time do you need to bid farewell to your current life and the people in it? Are you ready with the finances that are needed to live a full-time RV life? Would you need to have an "on the go" job while living the RV life? These are a few questions that should pop up in your head immediately before you can decide when exactly you can start this adventure.

Start with a To-Do List

You will have a long to-do list initially but listing things down which need your attention will always help you. The very first simple to-do list might look like this.

- Research about domicile residency

- Organize a garage sale to sell unnecessary things

- Research about health care options to cover your RV life

- Cancel utilities that you believe you can do without

- Research about campgrounds

- Research how to earn while on the go

- Start decluttering and minimizing

- Research about RVs

Your list will become more detailed as days pass by and you

start getting through while crossing off existing items off your list.

Simplify

While you are still living in your home getting ready for the departure date, start simplifying your life. Declutter your home and start getting rid of things that you don't need while you are living your regular life. Should you keep certain things in a storage unit if living on the road doesn't work out? Or would you like to go all in and only keep things that you are sure about taking along with you in your RV?

You are the best judge of what you want to do and therefore, give it a complete thought while you progress with the decluttering process.

Outline your Necessities

There's going to be a blast in your head while deciding what to keep and what should be given away. You will need far less than you think you do. Just know that you need very less than what you would need in a house made of sticks and bricks.

A few of the things that are indeed essential are listed below.

Clothing:

How much clothing you will require depends on the places you plan to travel to. Most full-time RVers tend to carve their route based on the weather, implying that during the summers, they head to the north or the west, and during winters, to the south. Living in mild climates would require you to have a few heavy and thick clothes. The following checklist of clothing should suffice your needs as a full-time RVer.

- 1 denim jacket

- 1 raincoat

- 1 pair of pajamas

- 1 wool sweater

- 1 button-up denim shirt

- 3 pairs of shorts

- 6 t-shirts

- 1 long-sleeved thermal

- 2 pairs of jeans

- 1 sweatshirt

As minimal as this may seem, you will realize that you do not need more than this.

Kitchen items:

While you are in your current home, take a close look at all the tools and utensils that make up your kitchen. Which of these can you not live without? Which one of these is actually eligible to make to the room you will have available for them in your RV?

Also, remember that having an RV means that there is a lot of shaking involved as mentioned earlier too. This shaking is equivalent to almost a 3.4 magnitude constant earthquake. So having glass plates and crockery is not really going to be a good idea for your RV life.

Minimal Decorations:

A few campers, if not all, do tend to have a spot for decorating their RVs while others like to keep their RVs elegantly sterile looking. You would definitely like to take a few things that would like to make your new mobile home appealing and inviting. For the interiors, small printouts of your favorite bands or movies make do for a good-looking wall. Your outdoor space will also need to be looked at. Whenever you move into a new location, the patio will become your most favorite space. Would you like a hammock? Foldable chairs? A portable grill? Solar lights for the patio? These are some of the things that will help you lie down peacefully and stay calm whenever you have settled in a beautiful location and plan to be there for a couple of days or more.

How to Increase Your Chances of Success

Start a Vision Board

There will be certain days during which you are preparing for the upcoming life on the road, and suddenly you will throw your hands up in the air and feel that everything you are doing to prepare yourself for life on the road isn't worth it. This is when a vision board will come into the picture and calm your anxiety.

A vision board will keep you motivated to reach the goals and targets that you have set for yourself. Make one by simply taking cutouts from magazines and newspapers and print some pictures from the Internet, which illustrate the kind of life you aspire to live.

Go for Trial Runs

Start with a few trial runs on long weekends or holidays before your actual departure date. Go out in your current vehicle and try to camp on weekends. Try to cook while you are out in the open. Spending more time outdoors will only help you gain more knowledge. The trial runs will help you decide what to take with you and what you can safely discard. If you already have the funds to buy an RV while living in your current home, transitioning could become even easier. Start living in your RV in your own backyard and enter your house only when absolutely needed. This will help you get familiar with the RV life without the real stress of traveling and "living" in some unknown town.

Joining an RV club

Why join an RV club?

There are many organizations that will make living on the road easy for you. RV clubs provide a community for RVers apart from other help. You will get discounts to campgrounds and even knowledge about events that are happening in the RV community. It's like having a live social network that keeps you posted about activities from other full-time RVers. It's a good idea to join these clubs and forums before you actually depart, so that you are aware in advance of the dynamics of the RV community.

Some RV Clubs to Join

There are a lot of RV clubs that you can join, which will make your life on the road as comfortable as living in a home made up of sticks and bricks. The most popular ones are listed below.

Good Sam Club:

This club has a community of over 1 million members and provides a lot of services. The club provides trip planning, which includes estimated fuel cost, route planning, RV services and rest stops that are available on your route. RV services include towing in the times of breakdown, insurance services for your RV and all your assets when you are traveling, etc.

RV Golf Club:

The membership for this club costs USD 99 a year. With the membership, members can park at many private golf courses and resorts for free. The locations are often beautiful and stunning, and there is no parking fee with the membership. In addition to this, many golf courses offer discounts to members.

Harvest Hosts:

This club is for those who love to spend time in the lap of nature. The membership costs about $40 a year that entitles you to park overnight in the parks of listed wineries and farms. They have more than 400 sites available at the moment, and it only keeps growing.

Escapees:

This club is expensive compared to other clubs but has a lot of benefits. The membership costs around $39.95 a year and there is no enrollment fee. This club has partnered up with several other RV clubs and offers shared discounts. The club already offers 19 five star RV campgrounds where members can hook up for $10 to $15 per night.

Passport America:

The membership for this club costs about $44 a year, and the main advantage is that it entitles you to a 50% discount to more than 1600 campgrounds. There are restrictions on the discount during weekends and holidays.

There are a lot of RV clubs in America, and most of them offer discounts to the same campgrounds; however, as an RVer, what you need to consider while choosing a club is which one offer greater discounts with additional benefits at a low membership fee.

Essential Items to Have

Your RV will need maintenance from time to time. Most of the small fixes can be dealt with if you have the proper tools and some amount of expertise or a data connection to Google or Youtube. The following equipment will come handy to keep a check on your RV's health.

Flashlights: It's always good to have portable lights on you when there is no constant supply of electricity.

Batteries: Even people who do not live the RV life keep batteries for backup. So, extra batteries will always be gold for your RV life.

Scissors: Because never has anyone felt that they did not need scissors. Scissors are always handy.

Fire extinguisher: You will be dealing with fire in a small closed space and even around while camping. Things can go wrong in a split second, and a fire extinguisher is a must.

Ropes: For times when your RV gets stuck in marshy terrains, and you need to pull it out or for any other general purpose.

Shovel: Always good to have. Multiple purposes while you are on the open road.

Water hose: It can be used to wash and clean your RV. It can be used for other purposes too.

Tool kit: A basic multifunction toolkit for the everyday American handyman to fix things.

Road flares: To be used in emergencies when you have a breakdown and need to draw the attention of passing vehicles for help.

Recycling bags: You are not just living in nature, but you are one with nature. It will become your responsibility to keep it as clean as possible.

Leveling blocks: You're not going to be always parking at a campground. You will have forest days, mountain days and valley days etc. These will come handy with the parking.

Propane: Makes for an important fuel to have at all times during your RV life. It serves multiple needs from cooking to cooling and heating your RV.

Duct tape: Well, a duct tape never goes waste.

Gloves: To help while you use most of the other essentials mentioned above.

Jumper cables: To jump-start your RV in case the RV battery goes too low.

Tire pressure gauge: To check the air pressure of your tires from time to time.

Light bulbs: Having a pair is always handy in case the regular lights inside the RV switch off in the middle of a journey.

Extension cord: To have a power plug available even a few feet from your RV. Good for those outdoor camping days.

Tarp: To cover your RV if you're taking a hike or are keeping away from it for a long period of time.

Sticks N Bricks to Full-Timers Transition Checklist

RVing offers a whole new world with unlimited possibilities of living a truly fulfilling life. Having all that extra space in the open, however, also means that you need to pack your stuff wisely for all the limited space within your RV. The essentials for a full-time RV life are listed below.

Eating:

For most of us, this would be the most important part of the essentials. Meals are an important part of the RV life, and you need to ensure that you have all the required material to suit your RV lifestyle. With sufficient storage for food items and ample space for cooking and cleaning, you could become a connoisseur of good food while on the move. Advance preparation helps too. Just be sure that everything is in place when it's time to put that meal together.

This list will help you with most of your eating needs.

- Cups: These will help you serve beverages when you have any visitors coming in.

- Mugs: Mugs can be used for any personal use, when you deal with liquid items or personal beverages.

- Plates: Plates can be reserved again for guests mostly to serve them meals.

- Bowls: Campers usually have their meals in bowls as it makes washing them easier.

- Small Utensils: These can be generic utensils such as a cheese shredder or a strainer.

- Knives: These will help with the cutting and slicing and even as a defensive weapon against animals or break-ins.

- Spoons: These can be kept in a limited quantity based on the types of spoons you may need.

- Pan: If you want to pan-fry any meals.

- Cleaning equipment: To clean up after cooking or eating.

- Napkins/Paper towels: To be used to wipe your hands and face.

- Soap for dishes: To wash those dishes sparkling clean every time.

- Sponges and rags: To help with the washing of dishes and other utensils.

- Tupperware: To store extra food from lunch or dinner for the next serving.

- Can opener: To open any can in case you buy preserved food cans.

- Bottle opener: To have that pint of beer or open any other bottle while you are camping.

- Oil for cooking: Essential to help you cook most of the meals during your RV life

- Condiments: To add flavor to your food. Again you can decide whether you want an elaborate set of condiments or whether simple salt and pepper will do.

Sleeping:

One of the most important things to a camping life is to ensure that you sleep well to have a fresh day ahead of you when you wake up. Keeping the RV windows open can let you breathe in the fresh night air, and you can also set the air conditioning to enjoy a comfortable sleep in any given weather. The following essentials will help with your sleeping needs.

- Pillows and pillowcases

- Sheets for all the beds

- Extra blankets and/or sleeping bags

Relaxing:

It would just be a regular apartment life if there were no room for relaxing and recreation in your RV life. Therefore, you owe it to yourself to carry the following items to keep you relaxed while you are on the road.

- Comfortable chairs: For when you spend your evenings outside the RV around a bonfire

- Novels: Novels and other books to read in your free time

- Card games: For when you have friends over

- Puzzles: To kill time every now and then

- Stationary: For making notes and to help with all the games

- Some outdoor games: A football or a soccer ball or some sports equipment for activities outside the RV

Bathing:

While you can enjoy bathing in lakes and streams from time to time while on the road, your RV will come equipped with its own bathroom and you will need to carry the following essentials along with you.

- Shower gel

- Shampoo

- Conditioner

- Toothbrush with toothpaste

- Towels

- Toilet paper

- Other toiletries

Outdoor Activities:

You chose this life because you love living in the open world without any fences. You will be going on hikes, camping outdoors in forests and truly living the life of adventure. Consider the following checklist for all your outdoor activities.

- Water bottles: To keep yourself hydrated while you are away from the RV.

- Sunscreen: Since the sun can be painful in the summers.

- First Aid Kit: Because you need to be ready for the smallest of accidents.

- Neck warmer: To be used on those cold days when the weather is cold but still beautiful for you to go for a stroll.

- Hat: To save you from the harsh sun rays.

- Sunglasses: Again to protect those precious eyes from the harmful rays of the sun.

- Shoes: Appropriate footwear for runs or hikes and other such activities.

- Insect repellent. Because out there in the open, the world belongs to everyone and not just you. So you will have other friends visiting you from time to time depending upon the area you are in.

- Backpack: To carry everything while you set off for any outdoor activity. To store your water bottles and light meals, your money and keys, and other important things.

- Gear for outdoor activities: Hiking stick, binoculars, camera, perhaps a tripod, a compass, an adventure watch, etc. Everything you term essential for the kind of hiker you are.

This is a basic checklist for every full-time RVer, and it may vary from person to person. When you actually set off into the open, you will get more comfortable with making your own list of essentials eventually.

Chapter Three: How To Buy An RV The Right Way And Save Thousands Of Dollars

RV Types

We have been talking about living the RV life through so many pages. Let's now get into the real deal and discuss the mean machines that are available in the market that will set you free.

Motorhomes:

Motorhomes are RVs that you can drive and come in a range of sizes, from basic to luxury models. Depending upon the make, their features and sizes are further categorized into the following types of motorhomes.

Class A Motorhome:

The design of Class A motorhomes is built around the chassis of trucks, or a specially designed motor vehicle or a commercial luxury bus. The front of this motorhome most of the times resembles a bus in design with the front being flat and vertical and the sidewalls having large windows. Its popular slide outs allow it to have a bigger area as compared to other RVs.

Class B Motorhome:

The design imitates that of a van, which has a raised roof. Naturally, it has a smaller area and is not wide like a class A motorhome.

Class C Motorhome:

The design is along the lines of a truck chassis and attached to the cab part of the truck. These are deemed as perfect RVs for all kinds of people. Whether you're singles, a couple or a family, class C motorhomes will fulfill your camping requirements.

Truck Camper:

These are known to be the most versatile type of RVs available in the market. Truck Campers are capable of going anywhere just like a regular pickup truck. In fact, they hook right at the back of a truck above the truck bed.

Popup Camper or Fold Downs:

Best for the new family that is just entering the marketplace of towable RVs. These have been used by families for camping over the years. Most of the times, Popups are the first choice of new RVers. Given their lightweight, they are towable by even the smallest of vehicles.

Travel Trailer:

These are probably the most common type of RVs you will get to see on campgrounds and roads around you. There are multiple floor plans available to suit every RVer's need. It can be easily towed by a frame or a bumper hitch.

Expandable Trailer:

Expandable RVs can be towed by medium-sized vehicles using a frame or a bumper hitch. These are treated to be similar to the popup camper except that they have sides that are of hard material in contrast to the tent material that comes with the popup camper. Consumers often treat these as an upgrade to popup campers given the sidewalls that are very durable. Many expendables come with a living space, kitchen space and bathroom and also slide outs.

Fifth-wheel Trailer:

These are the largest type of towable RVs. Large pickup trucks are used to tow these using a fifth wheel hitch. They come with large living spaces and can be easily towed because of their size.

Toy Hauler:

Toy Haulers are actually considered to be a sub-category of class C motorhomes. The name comes from the fact that it has enough area to actually accommodate your toys such as snowmobiles, motorbikes, ATVs and even certain four-wheelers.

Which Type of RV is Right for You?

Choosing the right RV for you can be a difficult task and scary given the investments both in terms of money and energy that you will be putting in it. For a first time RV shopper, you will be surprised and overwhelmed looking at the number of options that are available in the market. The following guide should help answer this question and make choosing your first RV a bit easy.

The number game:

If you intend to purchase a towable RV, payload capacity and tow capacity are parameters that you need to look at. Do not take wild guesses or rely on social media for this information as they can confuse you and misguide you by more than a mile. Get in touch with the vehicle manufacturer directly to understand these specs. You should also be looking at the weight of the towable as buying one which is not compatible with your current vehicle can be expensive and moreover, unsafe.

The number of beds you need:

Look for RVs with floor plans that will provide a dedicated bed if you are someone who will be spending most of your time inside the RV. You may feel that you can adjust even in a sleeping bag, but the frustrating experience of most RVers says otherwise.

The bath:

Decide the kind of bath you want. We suggest dry or no bath: This is a very subjective department. Some people are very particular about having a comfortable space for their bathing needs. Others are satisfied with using the baths available at campgrounds. Baths are an important aspect of RV life, and therefore, it is necessary to make up your mind about the kind of bath you need so that you have a good RV experience when you actually hit the road.

Decide if you'll want to boondock or camp all four seasons:

Some people would be on the road facing all four seasons and therefore go for RVs that support sustaining the weather of all four seasons. But if you are looking to boondock, make sure that you look for RVs, which provide a larger capacity to store fresh water and have bigger gray tanks and black tanks.

How much time you plan on spending inside the RV:

There's no perfect answer to this question as there is no right way to camp. Some people look for RVs with tidy bathrooms and cozy beds that will keep them warm through the winter nights while others might just be looking for a compact version of their concrete house that provides the minimal comforts of a home. Think of how much time you would be spending inside the RV and accordingly select a floor plan that supports that need.

Cooking in and out of the RV:

Again there is no right option to be selected here, as this is subjective too. Some people only cook in their RV kitchens while most others have never even turned their stoves on inside their RVs. Depending upon how much you cook, you should be able to decide on the kitchen space that you would need inside your RV.

Will you need to work in the RV:

Most digital nomads choose the RV life because it suits their work lifestyle. If you have to punch the clock, you might as well do it in a beautiful location, right? So if you intend to work on the move, make sure to select an RV with a floor plan that has one comfortable working corner for you.

The following questions will help you narrow down the search for your RV and set off for a life on the road eventually shaping your new life.

Should You Buy New or Used

This would be one of the first questions that pop up in your head when you have made the decision to buy an RV. Since we are mostly accustomed to buying new things all the time, most of us would want to go for a new RV. Also buying a used one can be scary for someone who is just getting ready to step into the RV world. What if there are repairs needed that you won't even come to know until you're at least a week into the used RV? What if you inherit a mess?

Let's talk about the pros and cons of buying a new RV first.

Pros:

Buying a new RV is like buying a new car or a new home. Everything is neat and smells good, and no one has ever used it before. Nothing beats the scent of "new."

A new RV also comes with a warranty. So anything that could breakdown will be taken care of by the manufacturer for a year or two, and you don't need to carry that burden on your shoulders.

Cons:

Going for a new RV will cost a lot of dollars. And the value of that RV will start depreciating the very second that you drive it off and if you plan to sell it later, the value you get for a resale might give you a heartache bigger than that of your first college break up.

Let's look at the pros and cons of buying a used RV.

Pros:

The main benefit is saving those dollars of course. If you are patient and good with your research, you may find a used model of the exact same one that you had decided to buy a new one of.

In addition to saving money, since it's been used, the chances are that the previous owners have installed some upgrades to the existing kit. This is like a bonus.

Cons:

The biggest con is that if the previous owners did not disclose any major structural damage while striking a deal with you, it would quickly turn into a major expense coming your way. A way to get around this is to get an inspection done, and if the owner is serious about selling, they may even be willing to pay for the inspection to get done.

The custom upgrades done by the owner may want them to try to get the money invested there back, which in turn may put the cost on a higher side.

The final drawback would be that a used RV may or may not come with a warranty. In such cases, you need to purchase a warranty plan of your own. Eventually, though, you will end up saving money on that warranty as compared to getting a new RV

Are You a First Time Buyer?

We've asked a lot of RV owners, and there haven't been many who've said that buying a new RV is the best thing to do. In fact, as your familiarity will increase with RVs, the more inclined you will get to buy a used RV. As we have already weighed in the pros and cons of used RVs, we see that there are hardly any major cons to buying a used RV if you have done your research well.

So if you have a financial crunch, don't worry, as it is completely all right to buy a used RV. At the same time, if you have enough savings and the thought of buying used things gives you a nightmare, you could very well go for a new one. The following are costs that are associated with a full-time RV life apart from the actual cost of the RV.

- Campground charges

- Extended Warranty

- Insurance for yourself and your RV

- Fuel costs

- Rationing your daily meals

So kindly factor all these in when you are buying your first RV to make your first RV experience as smooth as possible.

Securing the Best Possible Price

Buying your first RV can turn out to be a stressful experience. Here are a few tips that could help you secure the best possible price on your first RV purchase.

Let the dealerships decide which one you go to: If you have narrowed down on the floor plan, walk into different dealerships and inquire about the model you need. Tell them about how you have seen a similar model at another dealership for a lower cost. This technique will help you negotiate the cost of the RV that you actually have your heart set on. Negotiating is not rude. As long as you're honest, you should work to get the best price. The dealerships are well aware of what would be a good deal for them. Therefore, you don't have to feel the guilt on your conscience of buying the RV for a price that was lower than the proposed price by the dealership.

Don't buy on your first visit:

People who have worked in sales know that it's the best time to strike the iron when you walk in for the first time because that is when they get to work with your buying impulses comfortably. Let the salesperson know that they are not the only dealership that you are visiting. This calms down the salesperson and puts you in a better position to negotiate.

Watch out for that difference:

You may walk into two dealerships that are offering the same model for a difference of $2000 and naturally, you will want to buy it from the one that is offering it cheaper. Take a step back, and try to understand the difference in costs. Sometimes, you will realize that the dealership selling it at a higher cost is selling it with more benefits like a storage facility included for a year.

Try to get yourself a Gift Card:

Along with the purchase of an actual RV, you will also have the associated expense of the accessories along with it. Most dealerships sell accessories, and this is a good opportunity to negotiate for a gift card to get some of the essential accessories at the time of purchase.

Rent before Purchase:

RVs are very large investments, and a wrong purchase can end up being a costly mistake. Rent an RV of your liking and try it out before actually purchasing one to get a real-time knowledge of what you want out of an RV. All these checks will help you get the RV of your dreams for a price that would go easy on your wallet and make your heart content.

RV Insurance and Extended Warranty Plans

Just like regular vehicles, the law also requires you to have RV insurance and therefore, it isn't negotiable. The factors mentioned above should help you narrow down on the type of insurance plan that you would want to buy. Owning an RV can be a lot of fun to venture into a life, which includes travel, but it also requires a lot of investment and should be treated with care. The RV insurance depends on factors like the class of your RV, the amount of time that it is used for, whether you use it for limited periods or live in it full-time and other such factors.

The risks covered by RV insurance are similar to those for other automobiles. These include accidental damages, comprehensive cover and liability cover. Additional coverage can be bought for the other assets in your RV.

The additional coverage may vary from company to company

but mostly includes the following:

- Total loss replacement coverage

- Emergency expenses

- Towing and roadside expenses

- Full-timer coverage if you live full time in your RV

- Uninsured or underinsured motorists coverage

- Campsite and vacation coverage

RV insurance will help you protect yourself from spending excessive amounts directly from your own pocket in the events of theft or loss or any harm or damage caused to you or your RV in case of an accident. It also covers roadside breakdowns.

RV insurance cost will vary based on the factors listed below:

- The class and floor plan of your RV

- Your driving history

- Record of past accidents

- Whether you are a full-time or an occasional RVer

- The limits that are set on your policy compared to the deductibles

- Any additional coverage

How much insurance would you need on your RV?

The amount of insurance needed for your RV will depend on the factors listed below:

- The state requirements of the state you reside in

- The class of the RV that you will own

- The places you will be traveling to and whether this would involve crossing state or country borders

- Whether you want to use it throughout or occasionally

- Whether you have made any custom upgrades to your RV, which can lead to higher costs of maintenance and repair

Extended Warranty on RVs

Extended warranty for your RV is designed to cover the cost of repairs for the mechanical failure of a huge number of moving components within your RV. Most extended RVs usually cover replacement of full parts, labor, and even inspection and diagnosis costs. The contracts, however, exclude any damage or failure due to accident or weather and physical damage. So, if you look at the policies carefully, RV extended warranty can be treated somewhat opposite to that of RV insurance.

Is an extended warranty needed?

If we look at probability, 3 out of 10 RVs face major

mechanical expenses by their second year, and the number only goes to 8 RVs out of 10 RVs by the fifth year. If you work the cost of repairs, it's charged as much as $300 per hour between labor and parts and will only keep increasing in the future. With the level of technology going only up every day for RVs and the components installed in RVs, the expertise required for repairs is resulting in a raise in hourly labor rates and even the price of parts. An extended warranty will only keep all these costs in control and help you live a stress-free RV life.

Besides, RV warranties will result in huge confidence while being out on the open road knowing that you do not have to take the headache of costs or manually fixing the RV issues yourself and that there will always be someone dedicated to helping you through these issues.

We would highly recommend having both an RV insurance and an extended warranty at all times during your RV life. It will seem like an expense at the beginning of the cycle but will only ease your RV life in the long run.

Part II: Mind, Body, And Soul

"Traveling – it leaves you speechless, then turns you into a storyteller."[3]

Chapter Four: Emotional Aspect of RVing Full-time

Expectations vs. Reality of RV Full-Time

Ah, we are certain that everyone thinks that life on the open road is quite exciting and liberating. The freedom of traveling combined with the excitement of all the epic outdoor journeys that lay ahead sounds too good to be true. Well, fulltime RVing might sound quite fun, but it can give a beginner a rather false sense of reality when they start thinking about adopting this unique traveling lifestyle. Fulltime RVing is certainly not all peaches and cream, and the expectations of it versus the reality can be different. In this section, you will learn about the common misassumptions that people have about leading the RVing life and the reality of how it works. Irrespective if

---

[3] https://www.goodreads.com/quotes/508820-traveling-it-leaves-you-speechless-then-turns-you-into-a-storyteller

you are planning for a weekend getaway in your RV or want to take up full-time RVing, it is quintessential that you learn about the things that you can expect along the way. The RV lifestyle might not necessarily be all that you think it is and it is better to understand all this before you jump into it.

All RVs are the same

If you think that all RVs are created equally, then it is merely an expectation. The reality is that recreational vehicles are of different types and they come in various sizes and shapes. The term RV by itself doesn't mean anything. When someone says RV, what do they mean? Do they refer to a motorhome or a rig that's towable? Does it refer to a Class A diesel pusher equipped with all the amenities you need or a camper trailer that comes in handy for camping out in nature?

All the different types and classes of RVs that are available on the market these days can be quite overwhelming for someone who is new to the world of RVs, and it can be rather confusing. So, it is obvious that a prospective RV owner needs to do a lot of homework before selecting a rig that suits their needs and requirements. The kind of camper that you opt for will primarily depend on your needs and the RV lifestyle you want to lead. Do you want something that you can park in a camping ground and unwind with your family over the weekend or do you want something for you on your solo adventure and make it easier to get out there? Also, if you want to buy an RV you can reside in; you must ensure that the vehicle is adaptable to all climatic conditions so that it is safe and comfortable.

Apart from this, different styles and designs of RV rigs mean that they are all differently priced. The kind of RV you buy will depend on your needs and your budget. You can certainly find a used RV for about $15,000, and you can also spend a million dollars and purchase a custom-made RV! It is entirely up to you, and we are sure that by now you understand that all RVs aren't created equally.

An RV is like a luxurious personal yacht on land

RVs are at times referred to as land yachts, but remember that it isn't necessary that the climatic conditions around your RV are always serene. Don't get me wrong; there will be times when this is true! There is no better feeling than waking up in a remote camping site to the sounds of nature and perhaps that of water babbling in a brook nearby with some fresh coffee brewing over the campfire. That does sound perfect; however, this isn't always true. Sometime, you will wake up listening to noisy children from your neighbor's RV in the campground, or you might also be trying to drown out the other noises in a camping area of a music festival.

All RV Campgrounds are noisy/luxurious/*insert any other adjective*

Neither are all RVs created equally nor are all the dedicated RV campgrounds the same. RV campgrounds along with the experience they provide are quite varied from luxurious motorhome resorts to modest national parks; there is no such thing as a "typical RV campground." It is merely about finding something that suits your needs and your RV. From private to public campgrounds and boondocking arrangements for all those who are feeling a little adventurous to ultra-luxe motorhome resorts, there is plenty to choose from. There are different online forums and websites that you can check to find something that appeals to you.

RVing will make you outdoorsy

Oh well, as soon as you think about living the RV life, we are sure that you are thinking about something quite spontaneous, adventurous and outdoorsy. It certainly does offer plenty of opportunities for outdoor adventures, but you also have the option of merely sitting back and relaxing. According to your travel and vacation goals, you can do whatever you want to. The best thing about RVing is that you can customize the entire experience according to your needs and preferences. Camping in a comfortable RV- your home away from home, allows you to do exactly whatever you want.

It is intimidating to operate or drive

An RV is certainly bigger than your regular cars, and there is a learning curve when it comes to driving an RV. If you are used to driving sedans, then with some practice, you can easily operate a super-sized rig within a couple of days. Given the modern technology that is readily available these days, it is quite easy to drive and control the onboard systems of an RV.

So, it is certainly not as intimidating as it initially seems. The RV camping community is one of the most well-connected and ready-to-help communities in the world today. So, if you do feel like you are stuck, then you can easily access the roadside assistance that is available.

It doesn't mean saving money

You might think that RVing fulltime means instant savings, well this isn't true. The thought of dropping the mortgage on your home and shifting into an RV looks quite attractive, but living in a camping trailer can be quite expensive. The minimalistic lifestyle might lure you in, but achieving financial freedom isn't that easy. You will need to pay for campsite accommodations, maintenance of the rig, your day-to-day expenses, and the fuel bills! The one thing that works in favor of RVing full time is that you will have complete control over your expenses instead of worrying about fixed monthly expenses. For instance, a windfall from your tax return means that you can spend it on extra fuel, use it to explore a new destination or even spend it on renting a camping ground. The money is at your disposal and you can do whatever you feel right with that money. The only fixed expenses that you must be mindful of are the regular insurance and registration charges, and everything else is variable.

RVing fulltime means living in an RV park

Those who opt for the fulltime RV lifestyle tend to move from one place to another frequently and spend considerable time living outside in dedicated RV parks. They can dock on a friend's property, use services like Harvest Hosts to explore new places and so on. It is entirely up to you when you are RVing full time! You aren't bound by any rules, and you can keep making them as you go along! The travel videos online might make you believe that RVing fulltime means that you will constantly be traveling. This does sound exciting and might excite your inner wanderer, but that's again up to you. The chances are that you will end up taking a break from fulltime RVing from time to time to recuperate and prevent burning yourself out. This is something that you must give a conscious thought to. Are you interested in the RV lifestyle only because of its promise that you can keep exploring new destinations? Well, it is your choice at the end of the day. Fulltime RVing doesn't mean that you are on a fulltime holiday- unless you are retired. Even then you might have some work to attend to. Keeping up with the bills and all the other related expenses aren't an easy task. So, our advice is that you must carefully plan your finances before you allow the wanderlust bug to take control.

The Emotional Conflict of Pursuing RV Full-time

Living the full-time RVing life does sound fantastic; however, there are certain emotional conflicts that you must address if you are considering this lifestyle. All the videos and posts that you see on social media might make it seem like those RVing fulltime are living the dream. The images are real, the experiences will be amazing, but there are certainly other things that you must be mindful of as well. Challenges are a part of life and RVing fulltime is no different. So, here are a couple of challenges that you might face and the tips you can use to deal with them.

You will give up on your time

If you are RVing fulltime, then you will have to let go of your home. It can be rather difficult if you have lived in a place for too long. Letting go of the comfort of your home, familiar surroundings and all the things that you are used to can be tricky; however, you can certainly cope with it. The first thing that you must do is cut yourself some slack. It is a change and a tremendous one. So, give yourself some time to get used to it.

Leaving your friends and family

This one is tricky, and there is no quick fix available. Missing out on family holidays is quite likely along with any other important social occasions. You must prepare yourself mentally for the fact that you cannot meet your friends for a quick lunch or most importantly, meet them whenever you want. If you don't prepare yourself for l this, you will be quite distraught. The best thing that you can do is keep reminding yourself that your loved ones are always only a call away. You merely need to pick up your phone and call them whenever you need them. Don't allow guilt to get a hold of you. It will not do you any good. On your journey, you will meet a lot of interesting people, see exciting places and make some wonderful memories. Remind yourself of these reasons whenever you feel a little low. RVing full-time, especially if you are on your own will take some getting used to.

Loss of identity

Before you decided to opt for the RVing life, you were someone's co-worker, member of a book club, a manager at work and such. Sure, you will still be playing some of these roles, but things won't be the same. The roles, as well as the routines you were used to, are a part of your identity. At times you might feel that leaving your old life behind is equivalent to giving up your identity. It is okay to mourn this loss for a while. You must learn to be compassionate towards yourself and keep reassuring yourself that it is okay to feel that way since you and your lifestyle are undergoing a major transformation. Remember that things will always be fine if you keep telling yourself they are fine. Instead of thinking that you have lost your identity, think that you are working on building a new identity for yourself.

Dealing with relationships and loneliness

Working in an office, always being surrounded by people to living in a spacious home are things that you are probably used to. RVing fulltime means giving up on these things. It isn't necessarily a bad thing. This gives you time for self-reflection. The one thing that you must do is work on dealing with your relationships and tackling loneliness. The best way to handle your relationships is by often communicating with all those you love. Living in an RV can become like living in a pressure cooker if you don't take care of the energy that you fill the space with. There are different ways in which you can keep in touch with others, and you will learn about them in the coming sections. Apart from this, you can also join online communities to get in touch with other RVers to learn from their shared experiences.

The physical space

If you are used to living in a spacious home, then shifting into an RV will take some getting used to. Moving into a small space can come as a shock to your senses. Eventually, you will get used to it. This is the best way to apply the principles of minimalism to your life. You will have space only for the essential items and will not be able to hold onto unnecessary things.

Letting go of convenience and familiarity

You will certainly miss things like shopping at your favorite grocery store, visiting the places you regularly do and such; however, you must remember that one of the reasons why you opted for the RV life is because you want to be adventurous. Adventure does come with a certain price tag. If you love to travel and want to explore places, then this is a small price to pay. Again, this is where mental preparation comes in. You must prepare yourself mentally and emotionally for the change you are thinking of making.

Emotions

It can be rather confusing when you wake up feeling anxious, sad or restless and you don't know the reason. The sun might be shining bright, you probably had a good night's sleep, and even then, you might not feel like your usual self. This is quite normal, and it will happen on more than one occasion. So, you must learn to practice self-compassion, and you must start taking care of yourself. Use different exercises to alleviate stress. You can meditate; go for a walk or even talk to your loved ones. It is all about self-care; however, if you experience any negative emotions for too long and if it feels like they aren't letting up, then maybe it is time to take a break from fulltime RVing.

Tips for RVing with Pets and Children

RVing with Children

If you want to go RVing with children, then here are a couple of tips that will come in handy.

Choosing the right campground

You must consider your family's style of camping- do you like to spend time indoors or outdoors? Will you be more comfortable if there were planned activities? What do you feel about the availability of amenities? Different campgrounds and parks cater to different needs. So, ensure that you pick one that meets your needs.

Map out the stops

RVs are certainly big, so you must always spend some time on researching about all the easy-to-reach places where you can stop and take a break. A truck gas stop is a perfect place to park an RV. So, call ahead and make a list of all the stops you can make on your way.

Always plan for rainy days

Regardless of how efficient you plan for the family adventure, one thing you cannot control is the weather; however, you can certainly plan for it. If you are traveling with kids, then it is quintessential that you have a couple of plans for rainy days too. Carry board games, video games and anything else that you think your children will enjoy.

Using the space

You must learn to use the space in the RV efficiently. All RVs have plenty of storage if you use it properly. You obviously will not have as much storing space as you might have at home. So, you need to pack carefully and only carry those things that you and the children will need. Carry hangers to store clothes, drawers to store away the rest. You can also designate certain storage space to the children, so things are always in order.

A cleaning schedule is important

Well, cleaning up an RV is way easier than cleaning a home. However, since there is a space constraint, the small space can become messy rather easily. It means that you will have to keep cleaning the RV. To make things easier, you must always have a cleaning schedule in mind.

Don't forget to have fun! This is the most important thing. Plan, prepare and have fun! After all, that's what family vacations are about, aren't they?

RVing with Pets

If you want to go RVing with pets, then here are a couple of tips that will come in handy.

<u>Packing the right gear</u>

Before you can start RVing with your pets, you must make a list of all the items that you will need to take care of your pet's needs. During the trip, you can always add other items to the list that you wish you carried with you and then cross off all the other things that you didn't use. Doing this will make packing for the next trip rather easy.

<u>An itinerary</u>

It takes a little planning, especially if you are traveling with your pets. You must ensure that the RV Park or campground you opt for is pet-friendly. A quick Google search will help you plan the perfect itinerary.

<u>Start buckling up</u>

You might like the idea of sitting on the couch with your pooch or letting your catwalk around the RV. It might make the RV feel more like home, but this is quite dangerous for your pet and everyone in the RV. An RV can weigh more than 15 tons and driving such a heavy vehicle requires a lot of concentration. So, always place your pet in a carrier that you can secure in place or buckle them up with a seatbelt harness. This ensures that your pet stays safe.

<u>Coming home together</u>

Also, using a seatbelt harness or even a secured carrier ensures that your pets will stay safe and that they don't get lost. Place a pet gate between the RV's door and living space so that your pet doesn't escape. Also, ensure that the ID tags on your pet's collars are always updated and ensure that your contact information is included in your pet's tag.

Take breaks

Driving on the open road can be quite relaxing, but remember that your pet needs potty breaks and needs to go for timely walks. You can always stop at a park and explore the area with your pet.

Weather matters

Weather is one thing you cannot control. Ensure that you always follow the weather forecast and are equipped to deal with all climatic conditions. You are responsible for your pet's safety, so ensure that the weather doesn't become a problem. Keep a list of all the nearby storm shelters handy. Apart from this, ensure that you carry sufficient supplies for your pet to deal with hot and cold climatic conditions.

Be a good neighbor

Always clean up after your pet. You aren't the only one who is camping in the campground, and you must clean up after your pet.

Solo RVing Tips

Will I be alone? How will I be able to set everything up by myself? Will it be safe on the road? Will I be on the road a lot? What about my security? These are just some of the questions that will pop into your head if you are thinking about solo RVing. Well, don't you worry because we have certain tips that you can use to ensure that your solo RVing journey is enjoyable!

Design your own adventure

Perhaps the most important benefit of solo RVing is that you have the freedom to create your own adventure. You can decide the route; the destination and the activities you want to do once you reach there. When you are traveling by yourself, there are plenty of options, and you don't have to compromise! If you are interested in making a pit stop on the way, then feel free to do so! If you want to stay for an extra night at a campground, then you can do that too! You can create your itinerary as you go along.

Plenty of research

Before you think about a solo RV trip, you must do plenty of research. You need to research the routes you want to take and also look up the things you can expect along the way like the campgrounds, towns you will pass through, gas stations and weigh stations. Learn about how the RV works and ensure that it is properly serviced. Learn about certain essential repairs like fixing a flat tire or replacing a broken light. Make it a point that your gas tank is at least half full and carry some extra fuel with you. Apart from this, keep a couple of numbers for roadside assistance service handy.

Regularly check-in

Keep your phone charged and keep checking-in with your loved ones regularly. Keep sending them constant updates about where you are, the route you are traveling on and where you are headed. Apart from this, you must bring along an emergency tracker (so that you can be easily found in case of an emergency), a booster signal and a satellite phone. You should also carry your ID with you at all times and keep a photocopy of all essential documents like insurance, registration documents of the RV and your driver's license with someone you trust.

Never advertise that you are on your own

You will certainly be curious and excited to meet new people while traveling, but it is good to be a little cautious. Never give away that you are alone, especially when you have just met someone. Show some prudence when interacting with others and let your instincts guide you.

Arriving early

Since you are traveling by yourself, regardless of where you are headed, ensure that you always reach your destination when there is some daylight and not when it is pitch dark. Make sure that the office staff is still present at the RV Park or campground by the time you arrive. Make a list of places you plan on visiting or staying in and send this list to your family or anyone you think is right so they can keep tabs on you.

Follow these simple tips, and you will be fine on the road!

Managing A Relationship with Limited Space

If you are traveling with someone, then there are certain things that you must keep in mind so that the journey doesn't become unpleasant. It can be quite tricky to handle relationships given the space constraint. You will be sharing limited space with your partner while traveling, so it is essential that you learn to manage things. Here are certain tips that will help you along the way.

Don't stay hungry

Hanger is a real thing, and it can be the cause for a lot of bickering. A timely snack will prevent your emotions from getting the best of you. You will certainly be able to think better on a full stomach. Keep a couple of snacks handy at all times. In fact, a lot of fulltime RVers traveling with their partners think that hanger is one of the leading causes of unnecessary arguments.

Redefining intimacy

Since you will be sharing the RV with someone else, you need to learn to redefine romance. You don't have to worry about making any elaborate gestures. In fact, doing something as simple as brewing a pot of coffee in the morning and doing the laundry can be quite romantic too! It certainly isn't a fairytale idea of romance but remember that full-time RVing isn't a full-blown vacation and there will be chores that you must do. Learn to appreciate all the little things your partner does.

Managing your expectations

Social media can lead you to believe that full-time RVing is all rainbows and unicorns, but keep in mind that you are seeing someone else's version of edited reality. Learn to manage your expectations. If you have bookmarks of all the places you want to visit, then don't have any expectations until you see the place for yourself. Expectations often lead to disappointments and this, in turn, can lead to unnecessary unpleasantness. Instead, having little or even no expectations might pleasantly surprise you.

Establishing a routine

Space constraint in an RV is quite real. So, it is a good idea to establish a routine and assign roles! If you cook, then your partner can clean and so on. You both cannot be cooking and cleaning at the same time. If you do this, you will both be merely getting in each other's ways, and things will not get done. Also, establishing a routine brings a level of comfort with it.

Finding your tribe

You can always connect with other RVers and can form your own traveling tribe. Also, doing this will make you enjoy the alone time you get with your partner.

Keep track of your finances

Money is a touchy topic, and therefore, it is important that you stay clear and open about your finances. You don't have to be stingy, but it is a good idea to keep track of your expenses and savings. Fulltime RVing doesn't mean instant savings, and there will still be some bills that need to be paid.

Learn to let go

Learn to let go of petty arguments and petty misunderstandings. Take a moment to compose yourself before you say anything, and this can save you from a world of unnecessary grief. Also, you must learn to compromise. There will be certain things that your partner might want to do, and you might not want to. Learn to compromise and find some middle ground. Learning to compromise is essential for any relationship to work and traveling together is no exception. At times, it can be quite enthralling to step out of your comfort zone and explore things.

Start communicating

Remember that you are stuck with someone else in a small space for prolonged periods. This is quite different from living together at home where you can go to work, come back in the evening, spend some time together and then go to sleep. Fulltime RVing means that you are stuck with someone in close quarters all the time! Start communicating openly and honestly. In fact, this is essential to make any relationship work.

Time out

You must take some time out for yourself. It can be something as simple as going on a leisurely stroll or even sitting in a lawn. You will need some time for yourself to recharge yourself.

Decorating Your RV So It Feels Like Home

A significant benefit of traveling in an RV is that you can always have all the amenities you have at home with you while on the road. Road trips become quite enjoyable when it feels like you are traveling while sitting in the comfort of your living room. Here are a couple of simple ways in which you can transform your RV into a home on wheels within no time and without much of a hassle.

Wall décor

Perhaps the simplest way in which you can personalize any space is by adding some wall décor. The things that you can use for wall décor include photographs of your loved ones, inspiring quotes, photographs of the places you have visited or want to visit, some posters and so on. You can hang up anything that makes you feel good. You can do all this without worrying about drilling holes into the walls of your RV by using command hooks, velcro and even some putty. Another simple option at your disposal these days is to use wall decals.

Add some rugs

Most of the RVs have laminate flooring that is quite easy to clean and maintain; however, a bare, cold hard floor isn't quite welcoming, especially if you plan on living in the RV. So, a simple way to fix this is by adding a couple of rugs to the floor. Place a rug near your couch; add runners to your living space, a mat near your bathroom door and so on. You can quickly add some color and texture to your RV with rugs.

Put up some curtains

A valance makes the RV feel less like home and more like a vehicle. So, add some curtains and the space will look quite welcoming. You can use adjustable curtain rods for this; however, finding curtains of the desired length might not be easy. So, you merely need to purchase regular curtains and then alter them accordingly to meet your requirements. If there are a lot of windows in your RV, then putting curtains on all of them isn't a good idea since it will make the space seem smaller and more congested. You must opt for light colored curtains, and you need a staple gun to fix them to the valances.

Add some blankets and throw pillows

Adding blankets to the bed along with some throw pillows automatically makes the bed seem quite cozy and relaxing. If you have a couch in the RV, then add some throw pillows to it as well. This is a non-intrusive means of adding some color and texture to the living space and can make a lot of difference when you are trying to make the RV feel like a home.

Painting the walls and cabinets

This certainly is a bigger project than previous ideas. If you go ahead with this, then you will be able to transform the entire look of the RV's interior. Painting the walls and cabinets white will make the space seem airier and spacious. You can paint the walls and cabinets according to your preferences. Sticking to neutral and light colors for the walls and opting for hues of rich brown for the cabinets is a good idea.

Apart from all this, please ensure that you always keep the RV clean and clutter-free to make it more welcoming. Use the tips given in this section to transform your RV into a home!

ATTENTION: Planning a Camping Trip But <u>DON'T</u> Want to Spend a Fortune?

Here is **<u>just a fraction</u>** of what you will discover with the FREE bonus:

- Secrets to camping year round
- Choosing the ideal tent
- Finding the proper backpacks for your needs
- How to build a fire
- Camping with children

... and **so much more**!

Get instant access right now by clicking on the link below!

http://bit.ly/SecretsToCamping

Chapter Five: Being Social

Staying in touch with family and friends Back Home

RV Internet access is quite important and here are a few options that are available to full-time and even part-time RVers.

Dial-up, DSL and cable RV Internet access

An easy way for a sturdy Internet connection in an RV is to use the dial-up modem available at campgrounds and RV parks. Most of these places offer Internet access, but the network available is usually quite slow. You can also use the Internet access provided at local libraries or any of the other public spaces. This is possible only if you constantly keep traveling through towns and cities. Some of the campgrounds also provide phone and cable connections for Internet access and to activate them; you usually need to contact the concerned phone or cable company. If you plan on staying put in a campground for a while, only then will this option be viable to you. If this doesn't work out for you, then here are some other options that you can try.

Wi-Fi RV Internet access

Wi-Fi is certainly a major improvement for obtaining Internet access for your RV. You can get an adapter or a computer with a Wi-Fi card (802.11) to get Internet access. A lot of parks and campgrounds are also providing access to Wi-Fi networks that RVers can access. You can connect to the wireless hotspot that is provided in different locations like coffee shops, restaurants, convenience stores and such. The speed of Wi-Fi is certainly better than the dial-up Internet access. The range and speed will depend on the Wi-Fi network available and the configuration of the network.

Even if Wi-Fi is provided, you might not always be able to access all sites using the network. Apart from this, please check whether the Wi-Fi being provided is free or chargeable. Some places offer it for free whereas others have a charge.

Wireless or cellular RV Internet access

A 24/7 Internet access is quite essential these days, and even fulltime RVers are looking for it. More and more RVers are looking for Internet access even when they are boondocking or are staying parked in remote locations. The Internet is essential for various things like staying in touch with others, communicating, banking or even looking up direction. The simplest way to go about this is by using your cellphone or a wireless provider to obtain Internet access. Different wireless providers that you can choose from are Sprint, AT&T, Verizon and many more.

In the most rudimentary form, you can use a smartphone that's data-capable so that you can gain Internet access. Once the data is enabled on your smartphone, then you can also start using it as a modem for RV Internet access. To do this, you can connect to your cell phone's network by switching on its hotspot, connect the laptop to the smartphone using a USB cable, infrared or even Bluetooth. You can alternatively use a wireless router to provide multiple accesses. Ensure that your network provider has data plans that will meet your Internet requirements.

Another option at your disposal is to start using a wireless networking device like the air card provided by Verizon. This is quite similar to a USB device that you can plug into your desktop or laptop and then enable the data on it. It acts like a tiny portable modem and router. Once you connect to this network, you will have 24/7 Internet access. There are multiple service providers as well as data plans for you to choose from and choose something that will meet your needs.

Satellite RV Internet access

You can use a satellite system that's mounted on an additional auxiliary unit or even the roof of the RV. This certainly gives Internet access but is a rather expensive means of staying online. The satellite system that's used to provide Internet access is nothing like the ones that are used for TV; however, once you purchase a data or Internet satellite system, then you might be able to add the necessary hardware to accommodate a television.

The advantage of using satellite Internet is that it gives you the liberty to be mobile and even access the Internet whilst in remote areas that are outside the purview of your cellular network provider. Since you have the option of mounting it on the roof of the RV or any other auxiliary part, it doesn't take up any space.

On the downside, these services are rather quite expensive, are slow during peak hours, tend to have restrictive policies and weather can be your enemy. You need a clear sky to gain Internet access with this system, so a cloudy sky will not do you any good. The hardware essential for this setup can cost you at least $1300 and can go into tens of thousands of dollars according to the setup you are looking for.

Satellite phones

Satellite phones haven't necessarily been a cost-effective option in the past, but in recent years they have become more affordable. Satellite phones are akin to mobile phones that don't rely on any cellular network provider for communication and instead depend on an orbiting satellite to place any calls. The coverage provided by this is way more than that granted by regular terrestrial-based cell phone stations. According to the system that you use, you can gain access to certain regions or even worldwide access. This comes in handy, especially for all those who usually travel in remote areas with barely any terrestrial cellular network coverage. Purchasing a satellite phone is a good investment, and you can always stay in touch with your loved ones. These devices have an omnidirectional antenna that you don't need to align. As long as there is a line of sight between the satellite and the phone, you will never be entirely off the grid.

Making a voice call can be chargeable between $0.15 to $2 per minute. The cost of transmitting data can be rather expensive, and you can choose from several pre-paid plans available. Be prepared to spend a couple of hundreds of dollars if you are interested in purchasing one of the latest models of satellite phones; however, the earlier versions are not that expensive, and they still do their job. For instance, the 9505 A that was launched in 2001 retails for around $1000.

Talking to Other RVers and Making New Friends

Attending RV events

Different RV events are regularly held so try attending them if you want to make friends on the road. Not only will you meet new people, but it is also a chance for you to connect with like-minded people. If you are new to RVing, then this is one step that you must not skip. These events cater to the needs of solo RVers, those traveling with partners or even families.

Stay online

There is nothing like social media to meet new people. Not only will you be able to stay with your friends and family by using this, but you can certainly meet others too. There are plenty of online forums dedicated to RVing, pages on social media sites you can follow and even online groups that you can join.

Take the first step

Learn to take the initiative to strike up a conversation with others you meet along the way. For instance, if you are parked at a campground or an RV park, then you can always approach your neighbors and try to talk to them! You never know when you might make friends!

Chapter Six: Your Body

Medical, Health, and Dental Insurance for RVers

Fulltime RVers certainly have a lot of things to think about from finding the next destination to figuring out a route, the regular upkeep of their RV and so on. Apart from this, they need to call ahead and book their sites and find the necessary medical assistance. Another thing that they need to worry about is medical insurance. This isn't one of the most interesting aspects of RVing, but it is quite important. So, what is the best health insurance available for travelers who live in their rigs? How can you find the best insurance to meet your fulltime RVing needs?

What are you looking for in a healthcare plan given that you will constantly be traveling? If you aren't certain, then the first thing that you must look for is nationwide coverage or even international coverage. There are special plans for travel insurance that you can use for specific trips, but these don't work if you are RVing full time. Since you will be on the road indefinitely, you need a healthcare plan that meets your needs without an end date.

Most of the full-time RVers are either self-employed or freelancers. If you are one of them, then you need to buy health insurance for yourself. You can do this by enrolling yourself through the Affordable Care Act or Obamacare! A quick Google search will help you search for this plan, and you can easily get enrolled. Before you purchase the health insurance for your travel, there are some things that you must be aware of. The first thing is that the health care options available will be based on the state you reside in. So, if you are a full-time RVer or want to become one, then you need to make sure you have a health insurance plan. The second thing is that not all plans are created equally. Not every plan will cover everything you need.

What Happens If You Get Sick?

First, Be Prepared

You never know when things might take a turn for the worse. The best thing that you can do is be fully prepared for any situation. For instance, if you go camping and wake up with diarrhea one fine morning, what will you do? You need to drink plenty of electrolytes in such situation and maybe take the necessary medicines; however, what will you do if you forgot to carry these things with you? Well, that does put you in a bit of a pickle, doesn't it? Therefore, it is quite important that you are always prepared.

You must carry certain basic medications like the ones for flu, diarrhea, vomiting, fever and some painkillers. Apart from this, carry anti-allergens especially if you have any allergies. You never know when you might need an EpiPen! If you have any specific medical conditions, then carry the necessary medication along with extra supplies of it. For instance, if you have asthma, then carry the necessary refills and some spare inhalers.

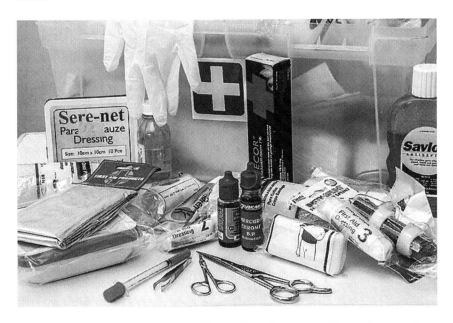

Apart from all this, you will need a first aid kit. A basic first aid kit must have a couple of plasters in different sizes, sterile gauze, at least two pieces of sterile eye dressing, crepe bandages, disposable gloves, tweezers, scissors, cleaning wipes (alcohol-free ones), a thermometer, sticky tape, cough medicine, eye wash, distilled water, antiseptic cream, cream for treating skin rash and insect bites and any antihistamine cream.

You can also download an app like Symptomator that works without Internet access. With all the technological advancements available these days, all that you need is an Internet connection, and you can easily reach a doctor online.

Carry electrolytes with you too. These are minerals that help balance fluids in your cells. You can always drink water to hydrate yourself, but nothing fixes dehydration like electrolytes. Electrolytes help hydrate your system quite quickly. Once your body is hydrated, you will feel energetic, and this is the reason why they are included in all sports drinks. Carry a couple of packets of electrolytes with you.

Getting Sick on RV Campgrounds

Well, there will be times when you might get sick in the RV campgrounds or parks. Before you decide to halt at any place, the first thing that you must do is plenty of research. Apart from researching the route, the places to visit and other places to make pit stops, you must also research the local doctors and hospitals situated in that region. Before you park anywhere, talk to the manager at the campground and obtain the necessary information about emergency medical clinics, hospitals, and doctors. It is quintessential for you to do this. If you have any allergies, please always carry your medication along with you. Apart from this, wash your hands often with a hand wash. Every time you head out of the RV and come inside, ensure you wash your hands. If possible, carry a small bottle of sanitizer with you at all times. If you notice that any of the RVers around you seem sick and if their illness looks contagious, stay away from them. If you catch anything that seems contagious or if it is diagnosed as being contagious, then avoid public spaces.

Getting Sick While Far Away from Everyone

What if you get sick when you are out camping away from everyone? If there are people around, it is quite easy to call for help; however, being isolated from everyone and getting sick is certainly not a good thing, but there are certain things that you can do to help yourself even when you are away from everyone.

Hydrate yourself

While you are camping, the one thing that you must never forget is to stay hydrated. You must never allow yourself to get dehydrated. So, carry a water bottle and ensure that you don't share it with anyone. Water is your best friend, so add some electrolytes to it to prevent dehydration. In fact, even if you are dehydrated, drinking water that's enriched with electrolytes will help stabilize your internal system.

Eat something

If you are sick, then you will end up losing your appetite. Even if this isn't the case, your body might not accept the food you are eating. Please ensure that there is some food in your stomach if not weakness will make things worse. So, try to eat even if you don't feel like eating or even if your body is rejecting everything you eat.

Do something

You need to keep yourself occupied with something to ensure that you stay conscious. Maybe you are waiting for help to arrive or are waiting for your fellow campers to return, regardless of what it is; you must occupy yourself with something. You can always play some games on your phone or tablet to pass the time.

Be smart

Never push yourself, especially if you feel like you are coming down with something. Don't ignore the warning signals your body is giving you. Take a moment and assess your body. If you are feeling under the weather, then ensure that you don't push yourself unnecessarily. Instead, make your way back to the campground or the RV and call for help.

Part III: These Ideas Also Require Your Attention

"Jobs fill your pocket, but adventures fill your soul."[4]

Chapter Seven: Making Money

Workamping

If you are tired of your 9-5 lifestyle and want to hit the road now, then you must consider workamping. Workamping refers to undertaking any part-time or full-time work while you are full-time RVing. This allows you to enjoy the travel lifestyle you want while generating income.

So, who are workampers? A workamper is an adventurous individual, couple or even a family who lead a lifestyle wherein they can combine any type of part-time or full-time work while RVing. The common misconception about workampers is that they are retirees who are working in a campground and

---

[4] https://www.adaptnetwork.com/inspirational-quotes/jobs-fill-pocket-adventures-fill-soul-jaime-lyn-beatty/

they work in trade for the RV site they are docked in. This doesn't necessarily have to be true.

There is a common misconception that workampers are just retirees who work in campgrounds, own a specific type of RV, and only work in trade for an RV site. Workamping jobs can be of any duration, and it is entirely up to you and your financial needs to decide the kind of jobs you want to take up. A lot of workamping jobs deal with the outdoor hospitality industry. You merely need to open workamper.com and review the job listings on it and apply for a job you think you can do. The first thing that you must do is make a list of your talents. Do you have a knack for public speaking or singing? Then maybe you can work as a tour guide or even as a performer for any local events. If you think you are good at fixing things and repairs, then you can always apply for the position of a handyman. Most of the workamper jobs don't necessarily require a special skill set. The jobs available can range from performing the services of a plumber, a driver, gardener or even a temporary secretary.

Remote Work: How to Find a Job Remotely

You can also work remotely from wherever you decide to travel to. Here are some options worth exploring.

Blogging

If you like to blog or write, then this is the best way to make some money from your blog. Once you decide to make some cash from your blog, you are no longer just a blogger. You are more than a blogger; an entrepreneur and your blog is your business. Have you ever been to a seminar where people give free advice to attract clients? Well, a blog is quite like one of those seminars. When you blog, you are providing your expertise and knowledge in the hope that you can attract readers and gain loyal customers. In other words, you aim to monetize your blog and use it as a mechanism to increase leads. Nurture the leads you obtain, and once they are ready, you can rake in some money. There are a couple of steps that you should to follow to monetize your blog. The first step is to set up a blog. The second step is to write good content that will earn your blog good traffic. The third step is to convert these visitors into email subscribers. The fourth step is to send good-quality content to those subscribers to earn their trust. The final step is to sell products or services that your audience will want.

Affiliate marketing

It might be difficult to sell a product or market a service, especially when you cannot reach your target audience. At times, you need different means to sell your products, or you might need to make some extra money. In such a case, you should opt for affiliate marketing. In affiliate marketing, a vendor sells their products or services with the help of an affiliate. The affiliate will help to market and promote the products to potential customers. It will help the vendor make a sale, and the vendor will pay the affiliate a certain fee for the effort they make. Affiliate marketing is quite prevalent these days. It can be something as simple as writing a review for a product or service on any social media platform.

Photography

If you think you are good at photography and enjoy it as a hobby, now is the time to turn it into a stream of revenue! You can sell your photographs online and learn to make money from it. You don't need to be a professional photographer to earn money from your photos. It probably might not rake in millions of bucks, but it is a great way to earn a passive income. Whenever someone selects your pictures and uses them, you will receive a fee. Books earn a royalty, and similarly, you will gain a fee. If you think you are good at photography but need a little more experience, then there is no time like the present to do so. The idea is to sell those photos that are in demand. The pictures need to be creative as well as entertaining. Photographs of landscapes and dogs might not sell much, and stock photo sites might not even agree to place them on their websites. The photos you click should be such that different businesses and webmasters can use them. Companies, as well as webmasters, tend to buy stock photos for their blogs and sites. You need a good-quality camera and the necessary equipment. If you want to turn your hobby into a source of income, then you should invest in good lenses and a quality camera as well.

Online workshops or classes

You can create online seminars or courses. These options are time-sensitive when compared to other ideas in this section. They even require more interaction. There are a couple of different ways in which you can make it flexible and convenient for yourself. The primary thing you need to do is select a time and set a date for the class that works well with your schedule. Once you do this, you can plan other details for your workshop. You can start a workshop about anything. You can even turn yourself into a self-styled life coach and offer advice to your viewers. Select an idea and think of the different ways in which you can turn it into a workshop that the viewers will pay to attend. Your work doesn't end there; you need to market the workshop as well. If you write a couple of e-books about the same topic, it will give you better publicity.

Tutoring

If you are good at a subject or topic taught in school from kindergarten to grad school, you can take up coaching. You needn't worry about geographical barriers since the course is online. You can offer tutoring services for literature, a foreign language, basic math, or anything that you fancy. You can set up your online tutoring program. You can efficiently work with students from different time zones as well. The only thing that you need to fix is your timings.

E-book or a white paper

You can transform all the knowledge you possess and the experiences you have had into an investment! You should spend decent time and energy to write an e-book or even publish a white paper, but it will be worth your while. Your vendor will take a cut, but apart from it, you can start selling your work almost immediately! You can write about anything you are interested in. You can write how-to guides, recipe books, or even papers addressing any of the current issues.

If possible, then maybe you can even negotiate a contract with your current employer to work remotely. Well, this isn't always possible, but it is worth exploring.

Creating a Successful RV YouTube Channel & Blog

Vlogging refers to video blogging and vloggers share their ideas, thoughts, routines, snippets from their daily life and much more. A vlogger documents their daily life and shares it on the Internet. It is done to gain the attention of the audience and for keeping them engaged.

The number of opportunities that come along your way will increase with an increase in the views that your vlog receives. One of the most popular platforms for vlogging is YouTube. If you have a YouTube channel with a significant number of followers, then the number of opportunities you have will increase as well. You should be consistent with the way you upload your vlogs and engage with your viewers; growth is bound to happen. When you are consistent, people will automatically start liking and commenting on the vlogs you post. The higher the number of subscribers and followers you have, the higher are your chances for landing promotional gigs.

The cinematography of the videos tends to make a difference if you are interested in becoming a successful vlogger. Essentially vlogging is about being innovative and being genuine in front of the camera. Notwithstanding that, what attracts a lot of people is a video of excellent quality. Shooting a quality video implies that your recordings must be splendidly shot, cinematography ought to be innovative and the content being shared is significant and enjoyable.

The narrating is likely the most critical piece of the vlog. If you want to get your audience hooked on to what you are offering, then the narrative needs to be engaging.. Your vlog or YouTube channel needs to be the perfect combination of a story, title, thumbnail, good quality video and engaging content. Each vlogger tends to have a different method of retelling the same story. Some of them tend to opt for long videos recounting their daily activities. They tend to share details of their day-to-day life carrying out regular tasks like cooking shopping or running errands. Well, since your idea is to start a travel vlog, then you need to include aspects of your travel life that you think your audience will appreciate.

One of the essential things is an incredible thought. It relies on the vlogger. Apparently, everybody has an alternate business-line, and everybody has their hobbies as well. What you are sharing should be a reflection of who you are. Vlogging is about inventiveness and also innovativeness. Try not to constrain yourself to a couple of thoughts that somebody lets you know for profiting off of vlogging. Continue researching and finding the new ways, however, don't forget to serve your crowd to start with, at that point consider profiting because toward the day's end, any individual who earns with vlogging, is somebody who began vlogging for enthusiasm and not to benefit out of it.

You can make money through affiliate marketing by promoting or reviewing products or services on YouTube or a blog. Reviewing products or services are more comfortable than to create new blog posts from scratch. Each blog post is created to build the authority of your blog in the search engine and drive more traffic to your blog. Sharing a product, event program or seminar can also be promoted on your blog or YouTube channel.

You can just begin profiting with vlogging by joining the YouTube partner program. It is the least complicated approach to start. Ensure your record is the grandstanding. Go to your dashboard and search for the adaptation tab to initiate it and follow simple steps to get started. When it's set, it may take a couple of days to get the endorsement, and you'll be ready. From that point on, you'll be profiting off of your recordings. Take up vlogging only if you are fascinated and passionate about it. You cannot fake enthusiasm, and you indeed cannot hold an audience if you don't like what you are doing. You can make use of your blog for promoting any particular product if you want to. If you have developed an affiliate marketing strategy or are selling the program for yourself, then you can certainly make use of your vlog for promoting the same. If you can hold onto your viewers and keep increasing the number of followers you have, then you are a step closer to obtaining sponsorships for yourself. You may have seen your most loved YouTubers discussing the products or the merchandise they offer through their online stores, and clearly, all the activity gets through their YouTube channels. Not just your merchandise, but you can make use of the same strategy for promoting any affiliate products as well. It is a good strategy for affiliate marketing and selling.

Chapter Eight: Legal Matters

How to Choose Your State of Domicile and Get Your Mail

You need to select your domicile state to establish your proof of residence, for mail forwarding, for insurance purposes and even for renewing your driver's license. So, how do you choose your domicile state? If you live in a specific city and live their fulltime, then you are the resident of that state. You also need to establish domicile as well. Yes, there is a difference between residence and domicile. If you live in a specific place at present, then that place will be your residence. Your domicile is your permanent place of residence- the place you wish to return to after your traveling sojourn. You can always have multiple residences, but your domicile will always be one. You need domicile for the sake of all your legal matters like paying taxes, opening a bank account, voting, renewing your driver's license and so on.

There are certain things that you must consider before you pick a state as your domicile. The state that you opt for will obviously affect the taxes you pay, the rate of auto insurance, your health insurance and pretty much everything else you can think of. Three states are considered to be domicile friendly for RVers, and they are South Dakota, Florida, and Texas. These states make it rather easy to establish and maintain one's domicile. Most of the other states require that you reside in the concerned state for at least 183 days in a year to call that place your domicile. This is the reason why RVers opt for those three states. If you are changing your domicile state, then it is a good idea to sever all ties with the previous state. If you decide to change your domicile to one state but have contacts (driver's license, voter registration, and an employment record and vehicle registration) in the previous state, then you might be caught between the two states and will be subjected to double taxation and other fees. Once you obtain all these documents in the state of your choice, you need to surrender the documents from the previous state.

Banking

Selecting a banking institution

Just because you opted for the fulltime RV lifestyle doesn't mean that you can sever yourself from the economy or stop being a tax-paying citizen. You will certainly be able to ignore a lot of bills, but certain expenses still stay the same. You will still have to file and pay for all the necessary state and federal taxes.

Handling your finances while on the road has certainly become quite easy these days. In fact, you can manage your bank accounts online. You can check the balance, access your funds, make deposits and even conduct transactions online. When you are thinking about availing banking services, there are a couple of things to consider like how easily you can transfer to any outside accounts (different country). If you set up accounts with multiple banks, then please ensure that you can transfer funds between all these banks. It is a good idea to keep your funds safe at various unrelated financial organizations, especially when you are traveling. If you are cut off from accessing a specific account, lose your ATM cards, or maybe the bank goes out of business, then you will be left hanging. To avoid this, it is best to place your funds in different institutions. This is a means of diversifying your risk and is quite similar to not placing all your eggs in the same basket.

Another thing that you must look for is whether the institution provides online access. If you are full-time RVing, then it will become quite difficult to take care of your banking needs if your physical presence at the bank is essential. You can always check the website of the concerned financial institution online to verify whether the services offered by them will meet your needs. Check whether the banking institution has simple policies about opening and closing accounts and whether they will they be handling all the concerned paperwork for you or not.

You must also need smartphone access. Most of the banks these days have their mobile apps that you can download on your smartphone and use it to perform any banking service. There must be ATM access provided by the bank for withdrawing and depositing money. It must also be easy to transfer and receive funds. If the bank meets all these necessities, then you can open an account there. Also, please go through their terms of service along with their fee structure before you select a banking institution.

Credit cards

A lot of people aren't in favor of credit cards, and that's a good thing too. If you aren't disciplined about your spending and aren't cautious, then your debt can quickly pile up, and you will be caught unaware. The fee charged by the credit card companies is quite high, and this will further increase your debt. So, if you do have a credit card, then ensure that you keep the transactions on your card as small as possible. Credit card debt is a vicious cycle to be in if you are not careful; however, there are certain advantages it offers as well. If you are prudent, then having a credit card can help. Making any bookings and reservations is certainly easier if you have a credit card. Most of the credit card companies tend to provide travel insurance for any accidents or disruptions that occur while traveling. Since you will be traveling indefinitely, you need something to ease the payments you make. Paying for services using a credit card is quite convenient. In fact, you can link your credit card to any monthly or periodic payments you need to make like insurance or utility bills. The amount will be automatically debited from your account and credited to the vendor. Apart from this, there are reward programs and concierge services that most of the popular credit cards offer. If you need to make immediate payment and have insufficient funds in your savings account, then a credit card will help.

So, carefully weigh in the pros and cons of owning a credit card and proceed accordingly.

Tax considerations

You have to take care of your taxes irrespective of the fact that you are staying in a state or are on the road! You not only have to pay federal taxes but certain state taxes as well. The state taxes you need to pay will depend on your domicile. You must consider different state laws wherein you need to pay some taxes like the state income tax, tax for certain work permits and licenses and the sales tax on services availed or products purchased. If you work in a specific state for a considerable time even if you aren't domiciled there, then ensure that the concerned state doesn't claim you as being domiciled there. You can certainly be a resident in multiple states but cannot have more than one domicile.

There are different federal taxes that you need to pay as well. The federal tax is payable to the government of the country, and the state taxes are payable to the government of the state you are domiciled in. We suggest that you take some time and research about the different federal and state taxes you are liable to pay.

Chapter Nine: How To Plan Your RV Trips And Top Destinations

Where to Captain?

It is necessary to decide where and why you want to visit especially for people who are beginners to the world of RV. This chapter will help you choose a place that will be best for you.

Where Do You Want to Travel?

The first thing to choose is what sort of places you want to travel to. Do you want to explore bigger cities or do you want to visit remote places etc. The place you want to visit will affect a lot of decisions, the foremost being what sort of vehicle you need to buy. For instance, if you plan to visit big cities, you should buy a small trailer instead of a bigger machine. If you want to visit open roads then investing in a bigger setup is a viable option. You should also check the rules and regulations of the places, as certain places do not allow bigger vehicles.

How Do You Want to Travel?

Many people do not realize that people like to travel in

different ways. If you are more interested in enjoying the outside world, then it is recommended to choose a smaller vehicle. If you want to enjoy all the comforts of your home while living outside then investing in a bigger option will be better.

How Much Space Do You Need?

This question cannot be answered until you get out on the road. Some people think that they can handle living in a small setup; however, once they hit the road, they soon realize that they need a bigger place. To help you make this decision, consult with expert RV campers and RV superstores. These people can help you have a vision of what sort of setup will be the best for you.

How Much Can You Spend?

Another thing that you need to consider while choosing a suitable place is how much you can spend. This is an individualistic option, and everyone's budget as well as will to pay is different. Do not visit a place that is out of your budget.

How Comfortable Are You Pulling a Camper?

Adjusting to the RV life takes some time and learning how to maneuver one takes time as well. Whether your vehicle is small or large, it will take time to learn how to drive, park and back it up. If you do not feel comfortable about driving it on your own, it is recommended to join an RV school that can help you learn how to drive one carefully. This is essential for people who want to visit places that are considered to be risky.

Where to Camp in Your RV

When you hear the word RV, what is the first image that comes to your mind? Is it spending a dream week at a peaceful, serene and solitary campsite? Or is it a fun, busy RV park with new friends and fascinating conversations around campfires? The images might be different; however, the main aspect of an RV camping trip is always to enjoy and have fun. RV camping has something for everyone if you know how to find it.

There are numerous camping options available for every budget; for instance, some options such as RV resorts can be quite expensive; however certain other options such as boondocking are free.

Let us have a look at some of the most common camping sites and why you should choose them.

RV Parks

RV parks are one of the most popular sites for camping. These are privately owned campgrounds that are specifically designed for RV campers. RV parks offer either partial or full hookups. Full hookups allow you to enjoy unlimited electricity, water and sewage services. In partial hookups, everything is available except sewage services.

RV parks are easily accessible. You can easily get in and get out of these parks, as they are located near major highways. Many RV parks also offer other services such as free Wi-Fi and on-site laundry. RV parks that are popular with families also offer planned activities for children, game rooms, hiking trails, mini-golf, horse rides, pool, kayaking and other related activities.

While RV parks are a great way to enjoy your holiday without forgoing the comforts and pleasure, not everyone loves them. RV parks are often crowded throughout the year, and they are especially crowded in summers. Parks that are located near crowded cities are often packed in the vacation season. There is often very less place between two rigs, and it may feel too congested to many.

How to Find RV Parks

Finding an RV park and reserving it is quite simple, as there are many services and websites that can help you to do so. Reserve America is a great service through which you cannot only find an RV park but can also reserve a place as well. It is recommended to check the reviews of the park before reserving it on RV Park Reviews.

For frequent campers, buying the AllStays app can be a great decision. It is available for $9.99, and every cent is worth it. Through this app, you can find all kinds of campsites, right from state rec areas to RV parks and even boondocking places. It also features other relevant information such as incline and elevation of the campsite, reviews of grounds, different amenities, etc.

You can also find out about RV parks by joining various clubs such as Good Sam, Escapees, Passport America, etc. These clubs have annual membership fees; however, through these memberships, you will be able to score huge discounts on various campgrounds throughout the nation.

State and National Parks

Public parks are a great option for camping. These places are good for people who love solitude, natural beauty and silence. If you desire to relax and get away from the hustle and bustle of urban life, you should definitely camp at a national or state park.

Finding a National or State Park

Finding a national park is quite easy as all national parks are listed on the National Park Service's website. Do remember that you cannot stay at a national park unless you have made a reservation. You can make reservations through two methods; you can either make a booking through the website or call at (877) 444-6777.

Finding and booking a state park is simple too. You can find all the relevant information on StateParks.com. All the state parks are arranged and organized according to states on this site.

Costs

The price of staying at a National park varies according to the park, the campgrounds, and amenities. It has been observed that prices may vary between campgrounds even if they are in the same park. For instance, the Great Smokey Mountain National Park has many campgrounds from the range of $14 to $23 per night.

If you are a frequent traveler and want to visit many national parks throughout the nation, then it is recommended to get the $80 Annual Pass. This will cover entrance fees to all the parks. If you are 62 years and older, you can buy this pass for $10. Seniors also enjoy a 50% (up to) discount on camping fees. If you are a member of the US military or are a dependent of US military member, you are qualified to get an Annual Pass. The Annual Pass can also be used at other parks run by other agencies such parks run by the U.S. Forest Service, Bureau of Land Management, US. Fish, and Wildlife Service, U.S. Army Corps of Engineers and Bureau of Reclamation.

The costs of state parks vary according to states, duration, the period of camping, etc. For instance, if you visit a state park during the peak camping season, then you may have to pay $20 to $45 for an excellent campsite at a popular park. You may also have to pay a reservation fee that may go up to $9.

U.S. Army Corps of Engineers Campgrounds

COE or Corps of Engineers maintain many campgrounds and parks in every state. These are quite secluded, as not many people know of them. They are pretty and are often free or at least less expensive as compared to national parks.

How to Find the Corps of Engineers Parks

Finding a COE park or campground might prove to be trickier as compared to state and national parks. You can find good books online such as the "Camping with the Corps of Engineers" (a reference book), which can help you immensely. In this book, you will find almost all the COE parks throughout the nation along with all the relevant information. Always call the managers at these parks to check whether camping is currently available or not.

Another service that can prove to be quite helpful is Ultimate Campgrounds. It is a great resource that can help you find public spaces in Canada as well as the USA. It is supposed to be the biggest public campground list on the web and has over 31000 listings. These listings consist of state and national parks, along with COE, Bureau of Land Management, and all other state and federally owned parks.

Other options of finding a COE campground include using RVCAMPING.ORG where listings of each state are provided. You can also search and browse Google Maps to find a listing. These parks are normally located near water sources so you can begin your search from such places.

4. Boondocking

Boondocking is another word for dispersed camping, which is also known as dry camping. In this method, you are supposed to camp anywhere but a dedicated campground. This is a broad category as it can include anything right from staying overnight in the parking lot of a retail store to camping in a desert without a person in sight.

There are many options and places that offer boondocking services. Here is a small list that can help you on your journey.

Federal and State Lands

You can boondock at any federal land if you follow the rules and regulations. The rules and regulations of each land are different and depend on the agency or the park. For instance, very few parks allow people to camp about 300 Feet away from a water source. Almost all parks allow campers to boondock for 14 or more consecutive days. After this period is over, you must move many miles away if you want to continue living in the area.

Very few national parks allow overnight boondocking. This is because national parks do not want excessive land impact. Authorities may ask you to move to a dedicated camp area instead.

Along with national parks, certain sites managed and owned by Bureau of Land Management too do not allow overnight boondocking. But don't worry, as there are thousands of lands throughout the nation where you can boondock legally.

As each park (or agency) is different, it becomes rather difficult to check and follow their rules and regulations as they are bound to be different as well. You need to contact the offices and admins to check their rules.

One of the easiest ways to find a free campsite is using the website freecampsites.net. This site has an interactive map through which you can search for the desired campsite in a jiffy. This site is also user-friendly as people post reviews on it that can help you decide whether you want to visit a certain place or not. To check whether you can access a certain camp or not, it is a good idea to buy a topographical map or, if you are tech savvy, download Google Maps and switch on the terrain model. This will allow you to check whether your RV will be able to go to your desired camp or not.

It might prove to be rather difficult to find boondocking places on state and federal lands, or the process might prove to be quite convoluted; however, it is a part of the process, and if you try to enjoy it, you will soon start to look at it through an adventurous point of view.

Private Farm and Ranch Land

It is also possible to boondock at private farms as well as ranch lands; however, you need to ask permission first. Many people will allow you to camp at their farm for a night or two if you ask politely. You can also find paid boondocking areas through websites such as Boondockers Welcome etc. There are many private owned land listings on this site.

Another website that can help you find good boondocking opportunities is Harvest Hosts. This is a membership site that enables you to access information about boondocking opportunities that include ranches, farms, wineries, museums, etc.

Another way to find out about a boondocking opportunity is by talking to the locals and enquiring. You may find hidden and solitary but pretty spots through this method.

Retail Stores

A lot of retail chains and stores allow boondocking. You can use these opportunities as a rest stop while you are en route to some other faraway location.

It is recommended to ask the store manager before parking your RV at their store.

How to Act at Retail Locations

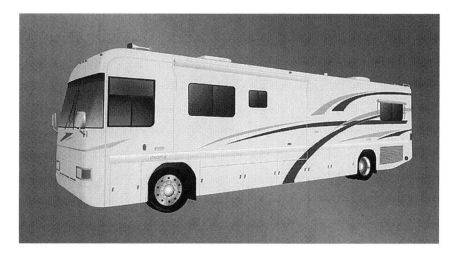

Many retail locations provide free overnight staying opportunities in the form of boondocking; however, you need to follow a code of conduct while staying at such places. Always ask the store manager whether it is allowed to stay at their store overnight. Do not park unless they allow you to do so. Almost all stores are open to people camping in their parking lots. Some stores do not allow you to do so due to the rules and regulations of the cities or towns they are situated in. It is always better and polite to ask for permission.

Always be discreet and respect others' space. Do not put out lawn chairs and start drinking. Stores allow people to park overnight as a courteous move; it is therefore recommended to keep it quiet and peaceful. You can repay the courtesy by shopping at the store and cleaning after you every time you leave a place.

Useful RV Trip Planning Apps

Smartphones are important for travelers as they let us keep in touch with our loved ones; however, smartphones are much more than just connection devices, and you can use them to make your trips extremely easy and restful as well. Here are some RV apps that you can use to make your RV experience smooth and delightful.

Yelp

Good old Yelp is a great service to check out reviews of various things and services. You will be surprised to know that it has more than 50 million reviews written by customers throughout the world. Yelp was primarily concerned with food-based services and locations such as restaurants, take-outs, hotels, dinners, etc. now Yelp has expanded its service to cater to various other locations. It is a wonderful app to find the best places near you.

AllTrails

This app gives the best choice to people who love nature and love to be outside. This app features over 50,000 trails and hikes all across North America. The information about these trails is not basic and is rich with pictures, tracks, reviews, etc. It also contains information about outdoor activities including fly-fishing, hiking, biking, etc. The app is GPS enabled so you can either find the closest trail next to you or you can also input data and find a trail in the nearby state. You can also track your activity to make a new trail and post it on the app for the use of others.

GasBuddy

One of the main aspects of an RV trip is gas money. Often people go over budget because they do not plan their gas buying strategies properly. GasBuddy will help you find the cheapest gas stations near you. You can also search for gas stations using postal code and cities. It is GPS enabled, and with a simple click, you can find the best gas place near you. If you find a gas station that is not available on the app, you can post it and earn award points. The app is currently available for Canada and the USA.

WiFi Map

Through this app, you can check the free Wi-Fi throughout the world along with their passwords. This app works offline as well, and you can type in your location and find good Wi-Fi close to you. It is a must have app for everyone who travels often and who likes to be connected all the time.

RV Parky

Through this app, you will be able to find more than 25,000

campgrounds, parks, Walmart's, rest areas, campgrounds, etc throughout the nation. You will also be able to check out the reviews and pictures of the places. It is a must have app for every RV enthusiast.

Passport America

Passport America is an old service that has been offering 50% discounts on camping club since the year 1992. Now it offers more than 1800 locations throughout Mexico, Canada as well as the USA. It is now free to download for members as well as non-members who want to browse through the list of RV Parks, Campgrounds, Resorts, etc.

SatFinder

This tool is essential if you want to set up your satellite dish, as it will help you by pointing towards the strongest signal according to your GPS location.

Sandidumps RV Dump Station

This app will allow you to find dump stations all over the Internet while you are driving. It is GPS enabled, so it will help you find the closest station with ease. If you are planning to visit some other city, then you can also manually enter the city and locate dump spots.

Instagram

Instagram is one of the best photo-sharing social media app. It's an amazing platform to document your photographs and your journey. It will help you share your photos with your friends, families and even strangers. It is a great way to keep your life and moments of fun in a well- documented format.

Roadtrippers

While there exist many paid options for RV road planners, Roadtrippers is a great free alternative that is still potent and feature-rich. It will solve all your problems. It will help discover the best viewing and scenic spots, best eateries, hotels, rest houses, attractions and many more. You will be able to plan a new trip right from your app, or you can also plan one on the app's website roadtrippers.com and then sync it to your app.

Overnight Parking Finder (Android)

This app is available on the Android platform. Through this app, you will be able to find many free overnight parking spots in a nearby Walmart. It also has a turn-by-turn guiding system as well as a RedBox locator that can help you locate every RedBox in the USA.

Walmart Overnight Parking Locator (iPhone)

This app is available on iPhone and will allow you to locate overnight parking spots in a nearby Walmart.

Weather Bug

Weather is an essential aspect if you want your camping trip to be comfortable and fun. Through this app, you will be able to keep a close eye on weather changes and will receive almost instant alerts. It has a special Spark™ lighting alert that will calculate the distance of lighting. It will also help you save energy costs as it features a home energy meter.

Key Ring

With the help of this app, you will never have to carry a membership card or a loyalty card anymore. This app will keep everything in one place. This includes shopping lists, rewards, coupons, weekly ads, loyalty cards, etc.

RV Checklist

It is a great app for everyone who owns an RV and is forgetful. It will allow you to be well prepared for your trips and will make sure that you do not forget anything important. It will also keep an eye on your progress related to important tasks. You can make different lists according to your need.

RV Trip Wizard

The RV Trip Wizard (RVTW) is a planning application that helps combine different functions into one application. While all the features that this program offers can be found on other apps too, it is quite convenient to use one package with all the features instead of shuttling between multiple apps.

One of the brilliant features of this app is that this program enables you to calculate a reasonably accurate cost of the journey that you are about to go on. In fact, the calculations provided by it are more accurate than the ones provided by other apps like the Good Sam Trip Planner. The RVTP takes into consideration different costs of travel like the cost of fuel along with the average cost of fuel per gallon, the average cost of a campground or park for a night and the average cost of the meals on a typical travel day. Apart from this, you can also add a buffer for all the other miscellaneous expenses that you think you might incur along the way. The app allows you to customize different criteria (like the distance you are willing to travel per day, average cost of fuel per gallon, along with the mileage the RV gives) for calculating the travel costs.

The RVTP also allows you to prioritize the campgrounds and parks you will want it to display on the map. Most of the fulltime RVers happen to be members of multiple RV campgrounds and having these stops displayed on a map in the order of priority will obviously make things easier, especially while planning the route.

Another feature that makes this tool rather useful is that it displays concentric circles on the map that denote the driving range that you opted for. This allows you to choose any other campgrounds present within the driving range.

There is also a database of campgrounds along with their corresponding user reviews that you can easily access to assess whether a specific campground is worth taking a break at or not. Reading the user reviews also helps you understand whether a specific campground provides all the amenities you are looking for.

The annual subscription of this program costs around $39 and we think that this is more than a reasonable price to pay for the services offered.

All that being said, we still believe that RTVW can be further developed and there are some issues that must be fixed. For instance, the mile markers for rest areas and fuel stops on the maps are at times incorrectly placed or are even mislabeled. Even though the users can enter several details about the specifications of their RVs, the map that is ultimately generated is quite similar to a basic Google Map route and it is not anything special. Also, without internet access, you cannot use any of the features of this tool and it doesn't have the provision of offline storage of the maps. This isn't a navigation program and is certainly not a substitute for a GPS navigation system.

This is certainly a helpful tool that you can use while planning a trip, but there is scope for improvement.

Top Three Destinations for RVers

People often buy new RVs and get excited about traveling but then waste a lot of time and money in simple and boring places. You need to listen to experienced travelers and ignore hyped places. Only this will help you find the perfect places. In this section, let us have a look at three of the most popular RV destinations that are suitable for everyone.

One of the main factors that you need to consider before going on an RV trip is where you live. Other than this you also need to take into account your budget as well as time. These things will help you select where you want to go. To make a trip successful, you need ample planning, especially if you are a beginner. Few people in this world can make an impromptu RV trip successful. Ample planning will ensure a safe and leisurely trip.

Seasons and the climate are other essential factors that you need to consider before choosing a destination. An RV trip is basically an extended road trip. It is recommended to avoid tourist traps and big cities unless you love the idea of crowded places and the hustle and bustle. Mind you, these places are also quite costly. If you are like regular RVers and want to visit a serene, calm and scenic spot, here is a small list of top RV destinations in the USA.

Yellowstone National Park

The journey to Yellowstone National Park is as beautiful as the destination itself. On your way, you can visit various beautiful places such as the Bighorn National Recreation Area and Devil's Tower National Monument as well. If the weather permits, you can also visit the Beartooth pass where you will be able to get breathtaking and stunning views of the Grand Tetons as well as other many mountain ranges that are situated next to the Yellowstone.

You should always try to arrive in the morning at the campsite, as this will ensure you get a good place. While Yellowstone is a huge and scenic park, it has limited facilities and campgrounds. It is therefore recommended to visit early so that you can get the best place.

You should definitely visit Old Faithful, which is considered to be the Grand Canyon of the Yellowstone. You should also visit Paint Pots and geyser basin. If you love fishing, then Yellowstone is the best place for you. While hiking is a great opportunity to check out the beauty of this park, it is recommended to take care of as many wild bears to roam around freely.

Yellowstone may prove to be quite costly if you are not well versed with planning a trip. It is recommended to consult with an expert RVer who can help you make good and budget-friendly plans.

Once you visit Yellowstone, you would not want to get out of it, as it is extremely serene, beautiful and delightful.

The Black Hills of South Dakota

Black Hills of South Dakota are very popular with RVers all around the nation, as they not only offer beautiful natural aura but also a variety of activities and events.

It is recommended to set a base camp in the hills after which you can visit the Badlands national park and the Wall Drug. You can also visit the Rapid City and Sioux museum.

If you have ample time, you can enjoy wildlife, beautiful scenery, activities and fun at the Custer State Park. Custer State Park has lots of activities for every member of the family. You can visit hiking trails, campgrounds, museums, etc.

You should also spend some time in Lead and Deadwood. These two are small mining towns that still exist thanks to a bustling casino scene. Here you can check out old gold mines, old cemeteries, museums, etc. if you have enough time to visit the Pine Ridge Indian Reservation. If you are lucky enough you may get a chance to attend a Native American Powwow.

Mount Rushmore and crazy horse memorial are worth visiting as well. If you visit in early August, you will be able to witness the annual Sturgis motorcycle rally.

Custer State Park has ten campgrounds, four lodges, four fishing lakes, six hiking trails, two small museums, and a summer theatre. It also has a small church.

You can also enjoy panning for gold or hike and attend a barn dance. The Black Hills are the best place for beginners RVers.

Biloxi, Mississippi

Biloxi is a small place in Mississippi near to Florida. Many people consider it to be a smaller version of Las Vegas as it has many beautiful and exciting casinos. Along with this it also has antique shops, white sand beaches, and great seafood. The beaches in this region are clean and often less crowded as compared to beaches on the west coast.

Biloxi is also famous as a military town so if you are in the area around the 4th of July you are in for a treat. You will be able to witness a level of patriotism and love for the nation that is non-comparable to any place in the USA. If you have a National Park Pass, you can camp for cheap in this town. You may stay around the Gulf Island National Seashore which is just five miles away from the happening casinos. The place is pocket-friendly, and you will not overshoot your budget.

People love to visit Biloxi as you can enjoy at the casino, the food is great and you can visit various clubs as well.

Hurricane Katrina did cause some problems with Biloxi but it has been rebuilt once again and has returned to its formal glory. You can also visit the Katrina memorial in the town.

It is a great and scenic city to visit and is well worth your time.

RV Canada/Mexico

10 Things to Know When RVing in Canada

Canada is a wonderful place for RVers as it is extremely friendly, beautiful and culturally rich. It is also incredibly safe, and your trip will almost always go without a hitch if you take certain things into account and keep certain things in mind while visiting. Here is a small list of things that you need to consider before visiting Canada with an RV.

1. Border Crossings

Canada and the US have an international boundary, which is maintained by US Customs and Border Protection on the south and CBSA or Canada Border Services on the north. It is a simple border, and you can cross it in a couple of minutes. You need to be prepared in advance if you want to make this border crossing smooth and bump free.

Important items to prepare when entering Canada from the United States:

Identification: While a passport is the best form of ID, you should also carry a certificate of citizenship, a birth certificate, a U.S. Permanent Resident with photo, etc.

Children and Pets: You can cross the border with ease even if you have children with you, however, if one or both custodial parents of the children aren't with you, you must procure and provide a consent letter. You can travel with a pet with ease if you have the necessary documents with you. Pet and pet traveling is managed by the Canadian Food Inspection Agency.

Food and Alcohol: It is recommended to contact CBSA to check the current restrictions as laws do change frequently. There are certain rules and regulations about how much alcohol and tobacco you carry while crossing the border for free. After a certain amount, you will have to pay for these two substances.

Gun Laws: While it is okay to carry guns in Canada, it is not as gun-friendly as the USA. You can carry guns in Canada by contacting the CBSA, and you will need to do some paperwork before you bring along your trusty friend.

2. Monetary System / Banking

Sometimes Canadian money is called 'funny money' because it is very colorful and vibrant. It is also waterproof and is made of a special kind of plastic. Two coins called Loonie and Toonie are used instead of one and two dollar bills. Pennies are not used in Canada.

While US dollars are accepted almost everywhere, they are often taken at par. This means they are considered to be equivalent to Canadian dollars. This may incur you a loss, as the US currency is higher than the Canadian currency. The best way to avoid losses is by using a debit or credit cards to get each day's exchange rate.

ATMs and bank outlets are present everywhere and are simple to use; however, you may need to pay a small fee to use the devices. This fee varies according to the place and time. Canadians use debit cards a lot, so almost all retail stores and outlets will accept them.

While credit cards are popular too, it is recommended to contact your bank and inform them that you are traveling out of the nation so that they won't block your account thinking it was stolen.

3. Driving

You need to carry proof of auto insurance as well as a valid and current driver's license if you want to drive in Canada. US licenses and insurance papers are accepted in Canada, so you do not need to get new ones.

It is recommended to keep a close eye on the speed limit especially if you are not used to the metric system. You may get confused and cross the speed limit, which may result in a big fine.

There are central laws that are implemented throughout the nation; however, there are certain region-specific rules as well. Do not talk on the phone while driving or you will incur a huge fine. You may talk on the phone if it is on the hands-free mode.

Seatbelts are extremely important in Canada, and you need to wear seatbelts all the time. Children must be put into booster seats according to their bodies. According to certain laws, you cannot smoke in the car if children are sitting in it.

4. RV Parks and Campgrounds

Canada has many different types of parks as well as camping grounds available. Many first-class resorts are available for camping as well. You can also find rustic and natural sites for camping. Every region in Canada is distinctive and has different parks. Each park will offer you beautiful scenery and atmosphere. To find out more about camping grounds, consult the Internet or contact the local tourism office. You can then formulate a plan that will help you cover a lot of spots in one trip.

5. Language

English is the most spoken language in Canada; however, French is widely spoken and understood as well. Certain areas such as Quebec are predominantly francophone; however, people often understand English just fine. Canada is a multicultural society, and you will find people from different parts of the world living together and speaking each other's languages. Hindi, Punjabi, Spanish, etc. are widely spoken as well.

6. Safety

Canada is one of the safest regions in the world; however, it is still recommended to stay aware and be smart about safety. It is always better to be safe than sorry. Don't leave your valuables easily accessible in your vehicle and always lock all the doors carefully. Remember, keep an eye on everything and never let your common sense falter. If you follow simple rules and regulations, you will be able to enjoy and finish your trip without any issue.

7. Internet and Cell Phone Coverage

Almost all campgrounds and RV parks in Canada offer Wi-Fi services. The certain provincial and federal campgrounds may not offer you this service as they are situated in remote areas. Internet service can also be found at cafes, libraries and downtown centers. Cellphone coverage is great except in remote areas. In remote areas, you may have to go without cellphones. It is recommended to check the roaming rates that are applicable in Canada with your provider.

8. The Metric System

Canada follows the metric system so everything from fuel,

weight, distance, etc. will be measured using metric units such as liters, kilos, meters, etc.

9. Restaurants and Grocery Stores

Many major grocery stores are available in Canada, and almost all American foods can be found in these stores. You must try certain authentic recipes of Canada in local farmer's markets and restaurants.

10. Planning Your Route

Canada is a huge nation that stretches right from the Atlantic Ocean on the eastern end to the Pacific Ocean on the west. You can visit various forms of nature such as beautiful coastlines, tall mountains, wide-open fields, the historical and francophone culture of Quebec, etc. It is therefore recommended to select and plan a route carefully.

RVing in Mexico

RVing in Mexico is considered a beautiful yet risky endeavor as people consider it to be horrendous. While Mexico does have a crime problem, the USA and Canada too have a lot of crime. There are certain areas that you need to avoid while traveling to Mexico; however, there also exist areas that are rich in culture, heritage, and beauty. There is something for everyone in Mexico.

Safety when traveling to Mexico

The first thing that you need to consider while traveling to Mexico is safety. You need to use your common sense while visiting. Do not stay at border towns for a long time and avoid traveling at nights. Do not wear fancy jewelry and avoid displaying a lot of cash.

Do not visit Mexico without any pre-planning. You need to sit and research roads, towns, and places you would like to visit so that you know the rough places and the desired places.

Crossing the US/Mexico border

The border crossing at Mexico takes longer than the border crossing in Canada. Make sure you follow the proper procedure. While some border crossings can happen considerably quickly, some may take more than an hour. It is recommended to cross the border early morning so that you can drive throughout the day.

If you travel within the free trade zone or within border zone then you will not have to undergo the border crossing procedures, however, if you wish to cross these zones, then you must follow them.

Note: Always cancel the vehicle temporary importation permit at customs when you leave Mexico.

Documents that you need for traveling to Mexico include the following:

- Your Passport

- A tourist card, which is obtainable at the border

- Vehicle Registration Certificate

- Driver's License

- Mexican Insurance (Get it before the border)

- International Credit Card (should be in the name of the driver)

Vehicle insurance for travel to Mexico

You need to get Mexican vehicle insurance in Mexico as your American and Canadian insurance won't work. Conduct some research before choosing a vehicle insurance plan and service

Highway driving in Mexico

Roads in Mexico are of different styles right from toll roads to dirty streets. It is recommended to learn the rules of driving in Mexico.

Mexican roads have topes which are bumps mandated to slow down the traffic. If you hit a tope on top speed, then it may damage your RV along with dismantling objects inside the RV.

Campgrounds in Mexico

There are many different types of camps and camping facilities in this nation. You can find secluded beaches, rustic forests and first-class resorts too. It is possible that you may have some problem with electricity in some of these places however nothing will be too difficult.

Things change quickly in this nation, and thus it is always better to check whether a campground is functional or not.

Mexico caravan tour

If you are hesitant about visiting Mexico, it is recommended to join a caravan. Caravans are great as they help you with everything right from border crossing to finding you a suitable campground and guiding you about the cultural and historical significance of the place you will be visiting. Caravans are also great for people who love to be around people and make new friends. This is highly recommended in Mexico as it will provide you security.

Mexico is pretty and has a rich culture; however, it is not for everyone to travel alone. Options like caravan etc. can help you commute in a safe manner and experience the heritage of Mexico. Always be safe while in Mexico and always make plans before visiting any place.

Insurance rebates

You will get a refund for the time spent in Mexico if your RV is insured by ICBC; however, for this, your vehicle needs to be out of Canada and the USA for at least 30 days. You will have to present the proofs of entry and exit dates and will have show how you were continuously in Mexico for 30 days. To find out more about the same, contact the ICBC.

Packing Lists for Your First Trip

Here are some packing lists that will help you pack all the essentials before leaving for a camping trip. It is recommended to print out multiple copies of these lists and handout one set to every member who will be joining the trip.

Packing List for RV Galley

- Knives

- Cups

- Mugs

- Tumblers

- Plates and bowls

- Spatula

- Mixing bowls

- Tongs

- Pots

- Pans

- Spoons

- Can and Bottle openers

- Chopping board

- Teakettle

- Toaster

- Egg cooker

- Colander

- Dish soap & cleaning products

- Aluminum foil

- Napkins and paper towels

- Sponges, rags, towels, potholder

- Ice cube trays

- Bag clips

- Campfire fork

- Trash bags

- Lighter/matches

Packing List for RV Bed and Bath Necessities

- Soap

- Washcloths

- Beddings and pillows

- Towels: Small and Large

- Hair products such as shampoo

- Toothbrush, toothpaste

- Mouthwash

- Flip-flops

- Tissue paper

- Toilet paper

- Deodorant

- Nail clippers

- Lip balm

- Tweezers

- Razors

- Shaving cream/foam

- Night cream

- Lotion

- Moisturizer

- Hair ties

- Brush

- Comb

- Antacids

- Laundry Soap

- Blow dryer

Packing List for RV Living and Recreation Supplies

- Maps: Road atlas, Paper maps

- Lights: Headlamps, Lanterns and Flashlights

- Fitness Equipment: Skipping rope, Yoga mats

- Sunscreen

- Hats

- Sunglasses

- Headphones

- Walkie Talkies

- Shoes (running, walking, etc.)

- Excess Water bottles

- Water Gear: Wetsuits, swimsuits

- Rain Gear: Umbrella, Rain cheater

- First Aid Kits: Small and Large

- Backpacks

- Insect repellants

- Camera gear and Camera

- Binoculars

- Beach blanket

- Office Supplies: Pens, Papers, markers, scissors, tape, etc.

- Chargers and Devices

- Books, Magazines, etc.

- Playing cards, board games

- Frisbee

Chapter 10: Bonus Chapters

Pros/Cons Of Buying an Ultralight Travel Trailer

Ultralight Travel Trailers are becoming popular thanks to their lightweight and easy to maneuver design. They are especially popular with single travelers who do not want to carry a lot of objects and things with them and want to pack light. Here is a list of the pros and cons of whether you should buy an Ultralight travel trailer or not.

Pros

- They are cheaper than other trailers.

- Ultra Trailers are built with lightweight materials such as thin walls, light frames, etc.

- These are very lightweight and easy to maneuver.

- They are suitable for seasonal use.

- Storage is optimized if used with a tow vehicle. Can be towed with ease using smaller vehicles as well.

- Certain new lightweight trailers offer other benefits such as dual pane windows, foam block insulation, furnace heated tanks, etc.

- They also have efficient floor plans.

- They are small so that you can adapt to a tiny space with ease; you won't need a lot of space to park.

Cons

- They are not good for people who want to do a lot of RVing.

- They may not work well in extreme temperatures.

- These RVs are not durable.

- They may sway with the wind due to their lightweight.

- They have less cargo capacity and storage capacities, so they are good for one or two people only.

- The waste tanks are outside and are exposed. In cold climates, you may experience freezing.

- May not seem comfortable to some people.

- Best suited for couples or singles.

It is clear that these trailers are not meant for everyone; however, if you are a single traveler who loves to travel alone and light, lightweight travels may prove to be a great choice for you.

Best RVs for Winter Living

Not all RVs are suitable for staying in a winter wonderland. Your RV needs certain features that will make it suitable and able to withstand wintry storms and cold.

Certain RVs are specifically designed in such a way that they can withstand even the harshest of temperatures. They can brave snowy conditions and subzero temperatures without cracking a sweat. In this section, let us have a look at some of the best winter RVs that will help you travel in style and enjoy warmth and comfort.

Windjammer 3008W Travel Trailer

Features

- Electronically controlled holding tanks

- Total trailer insulation

- Thermo-pane windows

- Fireplace upgrade

- The heated mattress in the master bedroom

- Maxxaire ventilation fan

- Vent cover

- Floor-ducted furnace

Lance 4 Seasons Travel Trailer

Features

- Insulated hatch covers (removable)

- Azdel insulation stops rot, mould, and mildew even if the trailer is exposed to wet conditions for a long time. It also makes the trailer soundproof.

- Water heater bypass

- Ducted heating system

- Dual pane insulated window with soundproofing abilities.

Forest River Arctic Wolf

There are two versions available for this vehicle, let us have a look at the features of both of these versions one by one.

Arctic Package

- Solar wiring and prep

- Upper Bunk Windows

- Outside shower

- Pullout kitchen tap

- Friction hinge doors

Extreme Weather Package

- Racetrack ducted air conditioning

- Arctic insulation

- Quick cool fan

- High circulation ceiling fan

- Insulated upper decking

- Heated underbelly

- Furnace

Jayco 327CKTS Eagle

Optional features include:

- Dry camping package

- Dual pane safety glass windows

- Sani-con turbo waste management system

- Second power awning

Heartland Bighorn

Features

- Furnace

- Insulated A/C duct system

- Single piece under-floor heating duct

Heartland LM Arlington

Features

- Bedroom reading lights

- Power tilt bed

- High rise coffee table

- Safe

- Stainless steel oven

- Backlit tile backsplash

- USB ports

- Soft tables

- A multiplex lighting system

- Along with these, you can also add alumni guard awnings, exterior TV, slide room awnings, bathroom fan, dishwasher, etc.

Northwood Arctic Fox

It is one of the most well-known and often used vehicles for winters.

Features

- Full tub with hiding away shower screen and bath skylight

- USB chargers

- Queen mattress

- Porcelain toilet with foot pedal

- Fan vents in the bedroom

- Shaded skylights in kitchen

- Extra large fridge

- Microwave

- Booth dinner

- Jackknife sofa with throw pillows

- Digital thermostat

- Smoke detectors

- CO detectors

- LPG detectors

- 19 inch LED TV with DVD player and Bluetooth

- 15-inch aluminum wheels

Keystone Montana

Features

- Free Flow Air conditioning

- Dual thermostat

- Remote sensor with a ducted second A/C

- 12v tank heaters

- Heated city water

- Heated exterior convenience center

- In-floor water lines

- Heated underbelly that is enclosed and insulated

- Dump valves (Insulated and enclosed)

- Holding tanks (Enclosed and insulated)

- Completely vented attic system

- Foam core straight-line heat duct system

- Auto-ignition

- Insulated roof

- Insulated slide-out floors

You can see that there are many different varieties of winter-suitable RVs that can help you stay in a winter/snowy area with ease.

Tips for Overnight Parking at Walmart

Once every while you need to park at Walmart and other retail stores, either because you are trying to get from point A to B or you are tired and need to take a break. In this section, let us have a look at some tips and tricks that will help you stay overnight at a Walmart.

Always Ask Before parking

Do not park in a Walmart until and unless you have asked for permission to park there. It is recommended to contact the store manager and ask his or her permission before parking. While almost all Walmart outlets allow RVs and campers to stay overnight in their parking lots, certain Walmarts may not due to local laws and rules. This may lead to an uncomfortable situation where people may ask you to leave as soon as possible.

It is recommended to call in advance so that you can check whether a place has space for you or not.

Use GPS

While Walmart is sprinkled around and is always less than a stone's throw away, you can always find a good place using your GPS and maps. Through GPS you can also find contact numbers as well. Always look for a Walmart Supercenter as they have more space to park and almost always allow you to park overnight.

Parking

Always park towards the side and avoid any main area. Do not let your rig become a matter of nuisance for the customers as well as the employees. Try to find low traffic areas and park there. A great way to check where to park is by asking the store manager. These places are also quieter as compared to regular parking spaces.

Be a good guest

Remember you are not camping in the parking lot, you are just staying or parking overnight, this means that you are a guest at the place, which is why you must act like a guest as well. Do not take out your grill or stereos and do not disturb the employees and the customers. Try to be as discreet and quiet as possible or you may be asked to leave. It is always recommended to clean after you and avoid littering as much as possible.

Be a good guest and buy some things from the Walmart you are staying at. These things do not need to be souvenirs. You can just buy daily stuff such as toilet paper, etc.

Safety

Always check whether the parking lot is safe or not. If you do think that an area is not safe, it is recommended to leave immediately. Avoid getting into confrontations and trouble. It is better to be safe than sorry.

Thus, these are some of the most common tips that will help you stay overnight at a Walmart with ease.

Best RV Waxes

One of the best ways to keep your vehicle in pristine condition as long as possible is by using good quality RV wax. If you own an RV, it is necessary to closely check its condition and health and upkeep it all the time. This will ensure zero-trouble journeys that you will be able to enjoy.

You need to do a lot of things such as winterizing the RV, changing the filters from time to time, etc. it is also necessary to wax it frequently to keep its shimmer and shine so that it does not look old. Use the best wax to polish your vehicle. It will ensure that it looks good and works well. With the help of wax, you will be able to protect your RV from damage and various scratches. A good quality wax can also provide some degree of UV protection. It can also protect your vehicle from environmental damage as well. Wax dries easily, so you do not need to worry about staining or any other similar problem. It is a good investment that lasts long.

There are many options available in the market, which is why it may prove to be quite difficult to choose an RV wax. Here are three of the best RV waxes that are great quality and will work best with any type of RV.

1. Meguiar's M5032 One-step Liquid Cleaner Wax

Meguair is a trustworthy brand in the matter of RV waxes. While it produces many different types and kinds of waxes, one of its best products is the M5032 One-step Liquid Cleaner Wax. It has been specially formulated for RV vehicles and is water and environmental damage proof.

One of the best factors about the M5032 wax is that it consists of various chemical cleaners. This means that not only can this wax can protect your vehicle from damage, but it can also fix present damages. It can tackle light oxidation, minor swirls, haze and scratches effectively. Its nonabrasive cleaning formula will clean your RV without harming it. It will also polish and provide your vehicle protection all at once.

It provides long-lasting protection from salt air, corrosion, ultraviolet rays, etc. Along with this, if you apply this wax regularly to your RV, it can protect your vehicle from the negative effects of oxidation. It is thus one of the best RV waxes that are suitable for not only gel coat RVs but fiberglass vehicles as well. It ensures that your vehicle stays shiny, vibrant and crisp for a long time.

You can apply this wax using a machine or manually with your hand. Application and buffing are effortless and will not take a lot of time. A problem associated with this wax is that it is prone to baking which means it may leave a residue if you apply it on a 'hot RV' or in excessively sunny weather. Just wipe it off as soon as you put it on to avoid this from happening.

Pros

- Removes debris and stains

- Is non-abrasive

- Can eradicate light oxidation, minor swirls, haze, and scratches

- Long lasting protection from elements

- The application can be manual or with the help of a machine

Cons

- Can leave residue if not used properly

2. Gel-Gloss RV Wash and Wax

Another great RV wax is the Gel-Gloss 128-oz. RV wash and wax. It is a good quality concentrated wax and wash. It is biodegradable as it contains no phosphate and is made using bar soaps.

It is a three-dimensional product so that it protects, cleans and shines the exterior of your RV with ease. It is a good option for people who love to take care of their vehicle and want it to look new all the time.

One of the best things about this RV wash is that it can wash and wax in one single, simple step. It can clean and wax all at once. It uses carnauba wax, which can protect your RV for a long time. It can also take off stains off your RV in no time and it won't cause streaking or water spots either. It is great for gel coat RVs, aluminum siding RVs, and fiberglass RVs.

Pros

- Biodegradable

- Highly concentrated

- Phosphate free

- Removes stains

- Does not streak

- Contains carnauba wax

Cons

- Packaging is subpar

3. Turtle Wax T-477R ICE Spray Wax

This is another great wax that is available in the form of a spray. It is a satisfying and impressive product with universal utility. It works on almost all surfaces including glass. It works well on all kinds of RV exteriors and can provide shine as well as protection. The application process does not take a long time because it is in the form of a spray. You won't need a lot of time or energy to spread this wax.

Another effective quality of this wax is that it can also provide water beading. It has great UV protection capabilities which means your RV's paint won't fade due to excessive exposure to the sun.

It is streak-free and offers a great cleaning protection mixture. It is waterproof and has anti-static properties. Along with this, it also has lubricity agents which allow for an easy application. It has a good formula and is thus better than regular wax.

Pros

- Is highly versatile

- Is suitable for various materials

- Can be applied quickly and without any efforts

- Water beading

- Can provide high UV protection

- Contains lubricity agents

- Contains anti-static qualities

Cons

- Does not spread evenly in the first application

These are three good quality waxes that can help you to protect your RV and keep it in an excellent and pristine condition for a long time. These waxes not only offer protection against environmental elements but they also remove present damages with ease.

Don't Miss Out! Last Chance to FINALLY Solve This Problem!!

According to Frontiers in Psychology:

"There is growing evidence to suggest that exposure to natural environments can be associated with **mental health benefits**. Proximity to greenspace has been associated with **lower levels of stress** and reduced symptomology for depression and anxiety"

Do you want to reap these **amazing health benefits** while making **lasting memories** at the same time all without killing your budget!? Download this book **now** to find out how:

http://bit.ly/SecretsToCamping

Conclusion

Thank you once again for purchasing this book. We hope it proved to be an enjoyable and informative read!

All the information that you need about living the RV life has been provided within the pages of this book. From learning about what fulltime RVing is like, to the different things you can do to prepare yourself for the journey ahead and dealing with the life on the road and taking care of all the other aspects of living the RV life.

RVing fulltime can be an enthralling experience, and you can either travel by yourself or with others. It is entirely up to you! This lifestyle offers you a great degree of control over things that you might not have in your usual life; however, please ensure that you are prepared to take the leap! Use the information given in this book to prepare for fulltime RVing.

Make up your mind so that you can get started as soon as possible!

Thank you and good luck!

References:

RVing: Expectations vs. Reality - RVshare.com. (2019). Retrieved from https://rvshare.com/blog/rv-living-reality/

Expectations Vs. Reality - Fulltime RV Living & Traveling - Drivin' & Vibin'. (2019). Retrieved from https://drivinvibin.com/2016/08/29/expectations-vs-reality-fulltime-rv-living-traveling/

Attell, C. (2019). 7 RV Living Challenges, Coping & Tips - More Than a Wheelin'. Retrieved from https://www.morethanawheelin.com/7-full-time-rv-living-challenges-coping-tips/

How We Stay in Touch While RVing | RoverPass. (2019). Retrieved from https://www.roverpass.com/blog/staying-touch-road/

Greising-Murschel, J. (2019). 10 Helpful Tips For Making Friends While Living Fulltime In An RV - Crazy Family Adventure. Retrieved from https://www.crazyfamilyadventure.com/living-fulltime-in-an-rv/

Agredano, R. (2019). How To Travel With Pets In An RV. These 5 Key Points. Retrieved from http://www.doityourselfrv.com/travel-pets-rv-easy-ways-fun-rving-favorite-friend/

How To RV With Kids (Without Going Crazy) | Campanda Magazine. (2019). Retrieved from https://www.campanda.com/magazine/rv-with-kids/

Burkert, A. (2019). Tips for Pet Friendly RVing with Dogs and Cats | GoPetFriendly.com. Retrieved from https://blog.gopetfriendly.com/tips-for-rving-with-pets/

5 Ways to Make Your RV Feel More Like Home. (2019). Retrieved from https://blog.campingworld.com/rv-basics/make-your-rv-feel-like-home/

RV Internet Access - Your RV Lifestyle. (2019). Retrieved from https://www.your-rv-lifestyle.com/rv-internet-access/

10 Tips for Full-Time RV Travel with Your Partner - GoRVing Canada. (2019). Retrieved from https://gorving.ca/blog/10-tips-full-time-rv-travel-partner/

Health Insurance Options For The Full Time RVer. (2019). Retrieved from https://smallrvlifestyle.com/health-insurance-options-for-rvers/

Here, S., Life, M., Guides, G., Blog, S., Us, W., & Posts, G. et al. (2019). Retrieved from https://www.thewaywardhome.com/6-ways-to-find-remote-jobs-while-fulltime-rving/

How to Enjoy the RV Lifestyle Now – By Workamping! | Workamper News. (2019). Retrieved from https://workamper.com/workamper-article/how-enjoy-rv-lifestyle-now-%E2%80%93-workamping

How to Create a Successful RV YouTube Channel? // 7 Tips to Drive Success. (2019). Retrieved from https://drivinvibin.com/2018/07/01/how-to-create-a-successful-rv-youtube-channel/

Ryan, S. (2019). 10 Best RV Wax Reviewed & Rated in 2019.

Retrieved from https://www.rvweb.net/best-rv-wax-reviewed/

Malczan, N., & Malczan, N. (2019). The Best Cold-Weather RVs for Extreme Cold | Camper Report. Retrieved from https://camperreport.com/best-cold-weather-rvs-extreme-cold/

Pros and Cons of buying an Ultra-Light Travel Trailer. (2019). Retrieved from http://www.rvnetwork.com/topic/116363-pros-and-cons-of-buying-an-ultra-light-travel-trailer/

Pros and Cons of buying an Ultra-Light Travel Trailer - Google Search. (2019). Retrieved from https://www.google.com/search?client=firefox-b-d&q=Pros+and+Cons+of+buying+an+Ultra-Light+Travel+Trailer

10 Things To Know When RVing in Canada - RVshare.com. (2019). Retrieved from https://rvshare.com/blog/rving-in-canada/

Features of RV Trip Wizard. (2019). Retrieved from https://www.rvtripwizard.com/features.php

68892196R00102

Made in the USA
Columbia, SC
11 August 2019